# Channels of Belief

RELIGION AND AMERICAN COMMERCIAL TELEVISION

# Channels of Belief

## RELIGION AND AMERICAN COMMERCIAL TELEVISION

**EDITED BY JOHN P. FERRÉ**

**IOWA STATE UNIVERSITY PRESS / AMES**

©1990 Iowa State University Press, Ames, Iowa 50010
All rights reserved

Manufactured in the United States of America
♾ This book is printed on acid-free paper.

First edition, 1990

**Library of Congress Cataloging-in-Publication Data**

Channels of belief : religion and American commercial television / edited by John P. Ferré. — 1st ed.
    p.  cm.
  Includes bibliographical references.
  **ISBN 0–8138–0639–9 (alk. paper)**
  1. Television broadcasting — Religious aspects — United States.
I. Ferré, John P.
PN1992.6.C513    1990
261.5′2 — dc20
                                          90–35006

# CONTENTS

# CONTRIBUTORS

**Robert S. Alley** (Ph.D., Princeton University), professor of humanities at the University of Richmond, has written *Television: Ethics for Hire?* and coauthored *The Producer's Medium.*

**Judith M. Buddenbaum** (Ph.D., Indiana University), associate professor of technical journalism at Colorado State University, has published articles on religion news in *Journalism Quarterly* and *Newspaper Research Journal.*

**Mark Fackler** (Ph.D., University of Illinois), associate professor of communications at Wheaton College, has coauthored *Media Ethics: Cases and Moral Reasoning.*

**John P. Ferré** (Ph.D., University of Illinois), associate professor of communication at the University of Louisville, has written *A Social Gospel for Millions: The Religious Bestsellers of Charles Sheldon, Charles Gordon, and Harold Bell Wright.*

**Horace M. Newcomb** (Ph.D., University of Chicago), associate professor of radio/television/film at the University of Texas at Austin, has written *TV: The Most Popular Art,* has coauthored *The Producer's Medium,* and is the editor of *Television: The Critical View.*

**Quentin J. Schultze** (Ph.D., University of Illinois), professor of communication arts and sciences at Calvin College, has written *Television: Manna from Hollywood?*

# ACKNOWLEDGMENTS

This project began as a seminar at the 1987 Speech Communication Association convention in Boston entitled "Religious Dimensions of Commercial Television." There we discussed our chapters with E. Sam Cox of Central Missouri State University, Richard M. Dubiel of the University of Wisconsin–Stevens Point, Ray Penn of Radford University, Deborah Petersen-Perlman of the University of Wisconsin–Stevens Point, Jimmie L. Reeves of the University of Michigan, Henry L. Smith of Olivet Nazarene University, and Tom Worthen of Ricks College. We then revised our chapters and, with the advice of James W. Carey of the University of Illinois and manuscript editor Pamela J. Bruton, shaped them into their present form. I thank all of them for their support and their suggestions.

# INTRODUCTION

A century ago, Edward Bellamy wrote *Looking Backward,* a utopian novel that portrayed the late twentieth century as a time of social harmony achieved through centralized world socialism. The picture he painted was as detailed as it was rosy. He described everything from community dining halls and clothing outlets—no one suffered from hunger or exposure—to industrial production. Socialism and know-how had conquered want and envy.

Unlike Marx's socialism, Bellamy's had room for religion. From the perspective of the late twentieth century, the interesting point in *Looking Backward* is not the existence of religion but rather the manner of its expression. Bellamy endorsed religious broadcasting because it was efficient and egalitarian. Here is how one of the main characters in the novel describes religious broadcasting:

> There are some who still prefer to hear sermons in church, but most of our preaching, like our musical performances, is not in public but delivered in acoustically prepared chambers, connected by wire with subscribers' houses. If you prefer to go to a church I shall be glad to accompany you, but I really don't believe you are likely to hear anywhere a better discourse than you will at home. I see by the paper that Mr. Barton is to preach this morning, and he preaches only by telephone, and to audiences often reaching 150,000.[1]

By replacing "telephone" with "cable television" and changing 150 thousand to 15 million, it becomes clear how uncanny—and conservative—Bellamy's vision of the electronic church was.

This passage from *Looking Backward* highlights two themes in mass communication research that are germane to the following set of essays. The first is the model of *centralized production of widely dispersed messages*. Bellamy recognized in this model of industrial organization great social and economic efficiency, hence the character's excitement over audience size. Clearly many televangelists use this model when they say that they use the airwaves and cables to preach the gospel to every nation. Bellamy and the televangelists are right, of course: telecommunications are efficient means of disseminating ideas. However, the centralization of the enterprise raises grave reservations regarding control. Relatively few organizations control the channels of electronic mass communications. In a commercial system, this restrictiveness tends to bias communication toward those ideas that can generate great financial support. Raymond Williams wrote that authoritarian systems control what *can* be said, that paternal systems control what *should* be said, and that commercial systems control by what can be *sold*.[2] The predominant religious broadcasters on American television are those who are willing to spend substantial time in fundraising. Virginia Stem Owens subtitled her book *Selling Jesus in the Modern Age* for good reason.[3]

If centralized production of widely dispersed messages, by definition an essential characteristic of broadcasting, raises the issue of control, then *Looking Backward*'s depiction of the *individual within the mass* highlights the problem of audience. The novel suggests that physical presence at a communal worship service is unnecessary and even quaint, a sort of holdover from the more tribal nineteenth century. Early observers of television like Edward J. Carnell recognized the benefit of broadcasting to shut-ins and others who were unable to attend church services.[4] However, as independent religious broadcasters increased their audience size, this rationale gave way to fear that televangelism was siphoning supplicants and their offerings from the local congregation. Ten

years ago, at a conference in Indianapolis, I listened to Methodist
and Presbyterian ministers discuss methods to recover the congregations and the funds they assumed they lost to televangelists. Although evidence from surveys suggests that religious television sup-
plements rather than substitutes for church attendance, the idea of
millions of individuals isolated with their television sets like deaf-
mutes smoking the same hookah continues to be disturbing.

This vision is disturbing because it is so insidiously
tyrannical. (It was Machiavelli, after all, who cited the ancient
political maxim "divide and conquer.") Persons in isolation do not
engage in dialogue or communal criticism. Because they do not
participate in the libertarian mêlée of truths, half-truths, and false-
hoods, they seldom question, refine, or vivify their beliefs and
values. Isolated television viewers permit the media to raise or ignore issues, to circumscribe them, and to interpret them in typically both-sides-of-the-issue fashion, as if social problems fit neatly
into binary computer models. Our isolated reliance upon television
fosters the insidious tyranny because we let religious and commercial television programmers frame our thoughts for us. We do not
talk back to television, as former FCC commissioner Nicholas
Johnson advocated; instead, we simply listen as it talks to us.

Those interested in religious thought and action should
keep in mind that most people do not watch religious television.
Religious television preaches a type of entrepreneurial individualism to a regular audience of probably no more than 20 million
viewers, less than one-tenth of the population of the United States.
By contrast, on any given evening, nearly two-thirds of American
households are tuned in to one of the three broadcast networks. It
is in commercial television, not the electronic church, that the most
important public negotiations of meaning and value occur. *Looking Backward,* as much popular thought, distinguishes religious
programming from secular commercial programming, but this distinction is more apparent than real. What we call the electronic
church or religious programming is certainly religious—its currency is religious myth and symbol, most often with a slant toward
fundamentalist Christianity—but as Gregor Goethals demon-

strated in *The TV Ritual,* commercial television is watched ritually and its programming employs icons and sometimes iconoclasm, all of which points to religious faith, albeit the faith of civil religion.[5] Because of its social importance and its religious nature, commercial television not only deserves scrutiny, it requires it.

Religion is a mainstay of network broadcasts. Religious authorities such as Pope John Paul II and Archbishop Desmond Tutu appear regularly on the evening news, in which issues of religion and politics, whether between Protestants and Catholics in Northern Ireland or Jews and Moslems in Israel, are covered as a matter of course. Religious characters also appear regularly in prime time on shows like "M*A*S*H," "Highway to Heaven," and "AMEN!," not to mention the movies that reappear every Christmas and Easter. And certain episodes have a predominately religious theme. Telly Savalas played a priest on an episode of "The Equalizer" which dramatized the themes of forgiveness and repentance. NBC showed "Father Clement's Story," a two-hour Sunday night movie about a Chicago priest who adopts a ghetto teenager. "Moonlighting" explored the secrecy of the confessional, and "Aaron's Way" portrayed problems of an Amish family leaving Lancaster, Pennsylvania, for California. These shows may not have a religious purpose, but they clearly have religious content.

Religion is broader, much broader, than the formal evangelicalism of the electronic church. There is more to religion than churches, synagogues, mosques, and their associated doctrines and heroes and villains. These are religious artifacts and characters to be sure, but these are not the only manifestations of religion in a culture. In a more basic sense, religion has to do with a "way of valuing most comprehensively and intensively."[6] Understood this way, even the most secular culture has religious dimensions. The religious dimensions of culture are in its pervasive values and the logic that connects them. One need only examine what the culture celebrates and routinizes to find them.

Not that the religious dimensions are always apparent. "Cosby" or "Dallas" or sitcoms or soaps seem to be secular with hardly a nod of recognition toward anything sacred. However, religion need not be formal or institutional or even recognized to be omnipresent. John Wiley Nelson illustrated this point through his compelling analysis of the belief system common to a variety of expressions of American popular culture.[7] The Gospel of Luke expresses the point more poetically when it quotes Jesus as saying, "If [my disciples] were silent, the very stones would cry out" (19:40). Taking the advice for party talk — avoid religion and politics — commercial television avoids the risk of losing viewers by operating according to what some commentators have called the least objectionable program factor.[8] However, like political ideology, religion suffuses communication, whether we mention the subject by name or not. Like all cultures, ours is essentially religious, even if it is not apparently so. For this reason, it is important to analyze key cultural industries. Because commercial television broadcasts religious messages, usually unwittingly but sometimes ostensibly, we have subjected this medium to a variety of analyses.

The first two analyses approach the religiousness of commercial television broadly. Quentin Schultze understands television as the great narrator of our time. Narrative, to Schultze, is a religious activity, because through narratives we define who we are and what our lives mean. We think of our lives as narratives and, by doing so, see ourselves as participating in our own stories and in the stories of others. Narrative, that is to say, is the way that humans structure experience. Although each of us has a unique narrative, we participate in the broader stories of society and culture. We take part in family histories, community histories, organization histories, and national histories. How those histories are constructed, told, and enacted — how those histories are lived — expresses the beliefs and values of the community.

The structure of the mass, the dissemination of hagiographies, as well as hymns and sermons based on sacred texts are all ways that narratives have confirmed Christian faith in the West. However, the church no longer propagates most of the narratives through which we understand ourselves. At least in the United States, the television industry produces them. According to Schultze, "television drama often functions in society as religious narrative functions in religious communities." That is, we as a culture accept the myths which infuse our televised narratives, given that the average household tunes in for several hours a day. In his exegesis of television drama, Schultze finds three myths reenacted consistently across genres: good will triumph over evil, evil exists only in the hearts of a few evil people, and godliness exists in the good and effective actions of individuals. By attending to televised narratives ritually, we define our sensibility.

Whereas Shultze looks for religious myths in the broad sweep of television narratives, Horace Newcomb pauses to examine the single episode to see how elastic a narrative formula can be in dealing with an issue such as death or afterlife. The popular appeal of television as a story system lies in its use of repetition, in its examination of the familiar. Television drama communicates meaning not only through its patterns but also in the way that novel issues are resolved in terms of television's patterns. According to Newcomb, when television deals overtly with religious themes, it does not treat them as entirely otherworldly. As a medium of formula and familiarity, it hardly can. Rather, television treats religious themes within the bounds, however broad, of human imagination. If commercial television can be said to have a theology, then it is of necessity a theology of immanence and not a theology of transcendence.

Because formulas are social constructions, it could be that television's religious slant reflects the beliefs of the subculture of producers and writers more than mainstream culture or the episodic nature of television as such. To broaden our understanding of the religious dynamics of commercial television even further, Robert Alley discusses the conclusions he has drawn from fourteen years of interviews with television producers and writers. Those who create the narratives that we watch adopt what Alley calls "democratic humanism," a position that lies between an anything-goes relativism on the one hand and narrow-minded religious dogmatism on the other. The one would deny any purpose or social responsibility in television programming; the other would deny any range to moral belief and behavior. Democratic humanism is more than a pragmatic response to an industry in the limelight of a pluralistic democracy. Judging by Alley's interviews, democratic humanism appears to stem from a heartfelt affinity to the Judeo-Christian heritage and a respect for social and cultural variety.

With Judith Buddenbaum's essay, we turn from the inclusive study of the production of television narrative to a specific element of programming: religion on network news. Reporters seem to have adopted a peculiar Cartesian dualism, splitting mind from body and virtually ignoring the mind. Thus the coverage of televangelists of late has focused on promiscuity and finance to the near exclusion of belief. Buddenbaum documents this feature as well as others. Not only do the networks emphasize events over beliefs, but they also cover Catholicism more than Protestantism. (Disproportionate coverage is not necessarily advantageous, though, because the networks frequently ridicule religious motivations.) Buddenbaum concludes that "the networks do not take religion news seriously nor have they improved coverage over time." Apparently, democratic humanism has its limitations in the newsroom.

Religious public service announcements (PSAs), or "telespots," would appear to be the primary way for religious groups to speak with their own voices on commercial television. For my essay, I surveyed station managers of commercial television stations to discover their criteria for selecting PSAs for broadcast. I found that religious PSAs have a fifty-fifty chance of acceptance and that station managers choose thirty-second spots that portray uncontroversial moral universals such as the value of family life. Religious PSAs that gain the approval of station managers are typically expensive, short, and bland. Religious groups that want to broadcast must be willing either to buy expensive minutes and half-hour blocks of time or to design their messages according to organizational imperatives. Religious groups can speak with their own voices on commercial television only at great cost.

Control of the public arena for religious expression underlies much of the material in this volume. Mark Fackler examines this topic directly in his analysis of religious watchdog groups like Donald Wildmon's. Although we might complain that monitors are myopic or prudish, especially fond of counting acts of immorality, we should acknowledge their democratic legitimacy and perhaps even the service they perform. According to Fackler, "If voluntary associations are indeed the primary units of responsible social change, the legitimacy of the role of monitors is self-evident. . . . Without the monitors, the viewer stands essentially powerless against network bureaucracy." The difference between Wildmon campaigning for clean television and the United Church of Christ fighting the racist telecasts of WLBT in Jackson, Mississippi, is one of substance, not of kind.

The essays in this volume recognize the central role that commercial television plays in the communication of religion. With *Looking Backward,* they affirm the potential of broadcasting to serve religious needs of the public. But with the benefit of hindsight, they also understand the technological, organizational, economic, and social constraints that shape the religious dimensions of American television.

# Channels of Belief

RELIGION AND AMERICAN COMMERCIAL TELEVISION

# 1 Television Drama as a Sacred Text

### QUENTIN J. SCHULTZE

$\mathcal{I}$n a short story entitled "The Lost Civilization of Deli," Jean Shepherd projects a future world where anthropologists excavate the ruins of the great North American culture of "Fun City," known previously as New York. Deep in the remains of a fallen skyscraper the anthropologists exhume the dusty contents of a gray metal vault, perhaps a sacred burial site. The interior of the vault reveals row upon row of reels wound with celluloid and labeled in small script, "TV 60 Second Commercials."

Months later in the laboratory the scientists determine that the film contents of the vault were strangely imprinted with images of special people—perhaps idols? Passing light through the rapidly moving celluloid, the scholars watch the icons magically come alive: uniformed dancers singing "We do it all for yoo hoo hoo!"; a group of sun worshippers dressed in outlandish pagan costumes of staggering immodesty chanting "Join the Pepsi Generation, come alive, come alive!"; three women in a repository confronting a uniformed guard who is trying to stop them from ecstatically fondling small white rolls with the admonition: "Don't squeeze the Charmin!" Soon the anthropologists realize that the find was far "more revealing than any of the poor fables and tepid myths these people had left behind, what they called Arts and Literature." Watching the drama about Charmin toilet tissue unfolding before their eyes, one of them exclaims, "Those tightly

**3**

rolled white scrolls . . . they were worshiping! Are you ready for a cosmic theory? . . . If we can find out what was on those Charmins, or what they were used for, I believe we would know what their civilization was all about, what they believed in. Do you follow?"[1]

Shepherd's story may be a bit farfetched, but its thesis is worthy of serious consideration, if not of a "cosmic theory." Understood in light of humankind's narrative capacity and religious nature, television serves a mythopoetic function, maintaining communal belief and shared values. Television is thus a prophet of popular religion in contemporary America. Because television is the major storyteller of our time, the critic should interpret TV exegetically, as the theologian interprets the themes and myths of sacred literature.

## Narrative and Humankind's Religious Nature

The capacity for storytelling is one of the most widely overlooked and underexamined aspects of human nature. Scholars frequently speak of humankind's abilities to reason and symbolize, to fashion and use tools, as well as to exhibit moral character. Each of these abilities, however, is sometimes claimed in some rudimentary form for animals as well. We might speak even more convincingly of humans as storytellers, since there is no evidence that other creatures share any capacity for narrative.

Human nature is linked closely to story, for we are not merely storytellers, story listeners, and story watchers but story interpreters and, most importantly, story doers. In other words, narrative is not merely part of our leisure time or one form of artistic expression but is the very mode of self-awareness and the very drama of human existence. Human life is the participation in stories — those tales spun for us, those we spin for others, and those in which we actually live. Biography is story, as is community life. Each of our lives could be a novel no matter how unexciting it may seem compared with those we view on television. By our very nature we interpret and understand our lives as narratives played out in the real world and recorded selectively in our own memories and in those of our friends and associates. Each of our lives has the imprint of a story in which we play the lead from beginning to end; our actions are the unfolding of the plot.

Narrative, then, is a natural way for human beings to structure experience. We are inclined to think of our lives not as mathematical equations or computer programs but as stories. Narrative is the dominant metaphor humankind uses to make sense out of its past actions and to guide its future actions. Our friends say "Tell us what happened" when they seek to know who we are and what we are like. Story becomes both a style of expression and a mode of interpretation. In literature, on the stage and the television, through cinema and ballad, humankind gives life a narrative shape, texture, and significance. Narratives organize our personal experiences, giving them a meaningful form so that they can be discussed retrospectively and prophetically. As Stanley Hauerwas says, "Stories are thus a necessary form of our knowledge inasmuch as it is only through narrative that we can catch the connections between actions and responses of man that are inherently particular and contingent."[2] Stories bind events and agents together in intelligible patterns, articulating the richness of intentional action that is purposeful but not necessary. As Horace Newcomb rightly says in his essay in this volume (chap. 2), television fictions enable us to imagine the consequences of actions. More than that, however, television narratives help us to imagine human action itself, even if we find the particular consequences depicted to be absurd or unbelievable.

Not surprisingly, religious faith and spiritual traditions usually are expressed in and maintained through sacred narratives. Unlike a mere listing of religious truths or an enumeration of moral commandments, religious stories are dynamic. Spiritual verities frequently survive best as stories precisely because narratives are general and thematic, not idiosyncratic and legalistic. Religious stories such as those contained in the Torah and the Bible are regularly reinterpreted for new situations and applied to novel human actions and situations which could not have been fully elucidated by the early writers of the narratives. Every Sunday, for example, Protestant and Roman Catholic preachers tell their parishioners the meaning of biblical parables for today. Moreover, sacred stories are best able to account for human origins, responsibilities, and destinations. As Johann Baptist Metz has argued, religious faith is necessarily communicated as a story because "the beginning and the end can only be discussed in narrative form."[3] Religious narratives have an inherent sacramental quality, suggesting the existence of a reality beyond the stories themselves. Martin Buber says that a "story is itself an event and has the quality of a sacred action. . . . It is more than a reflection—the sacred essence to which it bears witness continues to live in it."[4]

The importance of story for religious faith extends beyond the canonical writings. Through the ages much of the influential Christian testimony (devotional, theological, and philosophical) was cast in the form of narrative (e.g., Augustine and Bunyan). The Christian community, like humankind in general, lives by stories, often finding in them spiritual paths and expressing through them the great mysteries of life and the majesty of God. Humankind's consciousness is "entwined in stories," says Metz, and it "always has to rely on narrative identification." Even when the "relative importance of the magisterium of history has been recognized," our consciousness "cannot entirely do without the magisterium of stories."[5]

All stories share with sacred narratives the indispensable task of locating the action of the individual in a broader pattern of meaning and identity. Certainly every story is unique. As Hannah Arendt says, the only way we really come to know a person is through sharing that person's story; a person's biography gives us more of a sense of the true person than any mere description or lists of qualities, which almost always lose the uniqueness of a person in a type or character.[6] Television narratives are particularistic, as Newcomb claims; no two episodes or series are merely mirrors of each other. At the same time, however, a story links the uniqueness of its characters and actions to some broader expe-

rience and themes. Like sacred stories, other narratives also provide us with the understandings necessary, in Wittgenstein's words,
"to know how to go on" in the face of fate, anxiety, tragedy, hope,
and so on.[7] William Stringfellow writes in *A Simplicity of Faith,*
"We are each one of us parables."[8] Our particularness as personalities and physical creatures still points to our shared humanness.
Individual television programs similarly are evidence of the common beliefs and values of Americans in the late twentieth century.

Despite the influence of the Hellenistic world on Christianity, the church of Christ remained of necessity a storytelling
community. The gospel was never fully subordinated to argument
or reason, and theology was generally linked to the redemption
narrative described in the Scriptures. Although researchers and
scholars who are baptized intellectually in the Enlightenment often
consider the telling and interpreting of stories to be unscientific,
the appeal of narrative to humankind is universal. Regardless of
the epistemological limits of narrative as a method of inquiry,
storytelling, in its myriad of media and forms, still anchors cultures and communities to their common beliefs and highlights their
differences. In his study of Martin Buber, Ronald Arnett argues
that "freedom in community is deeply tied to the narration of its
own history." He believes that stories can provide a community
with a sense of its past and a vision for the future; stories steer the
members' lives in a common, virtuous direction while allowing "the
person to encounter freedom through his or her own uniqueness.
Freedom through narration invites a dialectic between the tradition
and the uniqueness of a person."[9]

## Media Scholarship and Storytelling

Although it has become quite fashionable for television
researchers to assume that popular stories are important and
worthy of careful analysis and interpretation,[10] most television
studies are not grounded in any *theory* of narrative or even in any
theory of communication or popular art. Most scholarship is epis-

temologically thin, driven more by an easily learned methodology than a stated theory. This is especially true of television criticism, which, even when insightful and cogent, rarely elucidates the assumptions undergirding interpretation and critique.[11]

Most television research has been based on positivistic theories and quantitative methods adopted enthusiastically from the natural sciences. The study of mass communication developed in the United States during the 1940s and 1950s on the heels of positivistic sociology and psychology. As a result, media scholars looked largely to the social sciences instead of to the humanities for their theories, concepts, and methods. In the process they usually discarded an important historical and philosophical link to the great traditions of rhetorical analysis and critical inquiry. In the United States, only the field of speech communication strongly maintained those links. Consequently, although there is some marvelous work on narrative by these scholars, it is virtually unknown by media researchers.[12] In the last decade American media scholars have established a few significant institutions to forge interpretive approaches to their areas of inquiry. Generally called "cultural studies" or "critical studies," the new approaches to studying the media look either to early American sociologists like Robert Park and George Herbert Mead or to the contemporary British and Continental philosophers Walter Benjamin and Jurgen Habermas.[13]

In Europe the interest in narrative seems to have stayed alive largely because of the more enlightened ideological critique of empiricism and because of extant folk cultures, which still value indigenous storytelling. Whatever the reason, European Marxists and structuralists are far ahead of American scholars in examining the role of popular narrative in culture and society. The British field of "cultural studies," generally associated with the Centre for the Study of Contemporary Culture at Birmingham, is particularly noteworthy.

Some scholars disdain popular storytelling, especially when it presumes to be art. In the humanities this disdain has taken the form of a classicism which considers itself above the critique of lowly popular art (even though many of the classics were the folk art of their day). In the social sciences it appears as a preoccupation with the pernicious effects of various popular artifacts, particularly the portrayal of sex and violence. In both cases scholars are advocating ideas which preserve their special academic status and social standing.


## Popular Story and Culture

The idolization of fine art in modern society is based on a number of false assumptions about the nature of art and its role in society. Two of them are especially relevant here: (1) fine and popular art are mutually exclusive categories of artifacts, and (2) fine art challenges existing human beliefs while popular art merely confirms them. These assumptions are frequently invoked as defenses for elitist views of storytelling and culture generally. Such elitist views regarding television wrongly suggest that popular drama is unworthy of serious study, and most importantly, such views obfuscate the mythopoetic functions of much popular art today.

Categorizing art into fine and popular ignores the history and social nature of human actions. Over the centuries the uses of and ideas about particular artifacts have changed as cultures and artistic communities have redefined the significance and purpose of art. The most important development has been the "museumization" of art—its separation from daily life, including the life of the church. The result has been the creation of various categories and typologies of art, such as fine art and popular art, which obscure real similarities and differences among artifacts and their uses and their influence on each other.[14] Moreover, such typologies typically confuse the intended purpose behind the creation of a work of art with the various ways artifacts are actually used. As David Thorburn says about the aesthetics of television:

> Homer's oral epics, the plays of Sophocles, Aristophanes, Plautus, even Shakespeare, continue to be experienced as narratives and as performances in our own day, but we fool

ourselves when we imagine or pretend that contemporary versions of such texts very closely resemble their original, communal enactments. . . . Even with the story forms of our own century and native culture . . . there exists a gap between our contemporary mediated experience of such texts and the actuality of their originating embodiments before audiences who regarded them as objects of use and leisure, no more valuable or artistic or historically instructive than the jokes and conversations and social encounters that comprised the ordinary blurred continuity of their daily lives.[15]

Today the museumization of art is exemplified by broadcast museums, where early programs are viewed on videotape in contexts completely different from the parlors and taverns where they were first watched.

This is not to argue that all artifacts are somehow of equal aesthetic merit (however one defines "aesthetic merit"). A television commercial is not necessarily as instructive or edifying or interesting or entertaining as a production of Shakespeare. Nevertheless, the rules for evaluating and experiencing art change over time as individuals, groups, and cultures redefine art and what to do with artifacts. The popular art of one age may become the fine art of another. In the United States, for instance, many upper-middle-class jazz fanatics now scrutinize the forms and structures of the music, elevating jazz into a fine art according to their criteria. In the 1930s jazz was "merely" the music of a minority and was widely criticized on moral and aesthetic grounds.

One of the most persistent myths about fine art is that it always offers new ideas or beliefs that the artist intended to be communicated. According to this view, we read great novels or attend fine plays because of the aesthetic insights and intellectual challenges they offer. We "consume" popular art, on the other hand, merely because it tells us only what we already know. This false distinction assumes that art is beneficial only when it educates or illuminates, when it enhances our sophistication or deepens our understanding of high culture. Actually, today's popular art is more in tune with the traditional function of art in Western society—the confirmation of religious values and beliefs. Only in the last century have these religious objects been almost totally separated from their religious context and thrust into the classification of fine art. Many of the great paintings, sculptures, and musical compositions of past centuries were created to enhance religious worship and reaffirm the popular religious beliefs of the day. Nicholas Wolterstorff writes:

> To understand the art of ancient and medieval South and Central America, the art of India, the art of medieval Europe, one must set off to the side our contemporary image of the alienated artist who has a prophetic insight to deliver or a stinging condemnation to issue to his fellow human beings, and one must instead see the artist as one who is allied in fundamental religious convictions with his community. The stories, the dramas, the paintings, the sculptures, serve more as an expression of the religious convictions of the artist's community, and to confirm that community in those convictions, than to lead it into new ones.[16]

Like most fine and especially religious art produced over the centuries, contemporary popular narratives frequently confirm existing beliefs more than they challenge them. Of course the immediate purpose of a contemporary popular artifact may be to employ existing beliefs in the service of a client or a sponsor—to maximize audience ratings, to sell a product, to increase box office receipts, and so forth. This is the primary difference between folk and popular art; popular art nearly always has a patron waiting at the bank and collecting at the cash register. But in no way is the mythopoetic function eclipsed; it is simply channeled in the interest of particular individuals and institutions. As Hugh Duncan has said, popular art often offers the audience the means to unquestioned ends—beauty, happiness, success.[17] Consider the typical commercial narratives: a handsome young man overcomes unpopularity by using a new toothpaste or mouthwash; a wife restores her husband's love by serving him "home-style" spaghetti; a homemaker squelches her feelings of inferiority after discovering the secret of her neighbor's "whiter-than-white" wash. In each story the audience is not expected to question the ends—popularity, love, self-esteem—even if the particular advertised claims about particular products appear to be outrageous. A spaghetti sauce will not lead to a harmonious marriage, but who doubts that serving the right meals will not help build a happy marriage? And who dares questions the goal of a happy marriage? Even commercials, as one form of televised narrative, invite our participation in the making and remaking of myths.

All categories of art can function mythopoetically in society and community. When cast in the form of narrative, they frequently project a human world that ritually illustrates our commonness as a people and affirms widely held beliefs. In this sense storytelling in the mass media is similar in purpose even to the lessons of life we impart to each other. All true stories, says Walter Benjamin, "have an overt or hidden use—a moral, a practical instruction, a rule of life."[18] Stories often display this aphoristic quality even when they are not intended to educate. Wesley Kort's view of the narratives of religious communities is applicable to such public storytelling: "A religious community retains and rehearses its characteristic words and acts to maintain its identity against those alternatives of vacancy, chaos, or evil power which seem ready to preempt their place."[19] Public performances of narrative, like worship services, instruct the community of believers and enable them to share the stories and their meanings.

Over the centuries Jews gathered around the Passover table and Protestants met in homes and churches to celebrate communion. Today television audiences meet in front of the tube for a symbolic enactment of the community's shared hopes and fears. James Carey develops this argument in his "cultural approach to communication," which he contrasts to the "transmission view." According to Carey, the transmission view, which is dominant today in Western societies, conceives of public communication merely as the sending and receiving of information or knowledge. The cultural approach, on the other hand, more broadly likens communication to drama or ritual. "Under a ritual view," he writes, "news is not information but drama; it does not describe the world but portrays an arena of dramatic forces and action; it exists solely in historical time; and it invites our participation on the basis of our assuming, often vicariously, social roles within it."[20] Carey believes that much public communication is best understood as community drama instead of telegraphic, information-transferring communication.

Popular stories frequently ritualize the values, beliefs, and even the sensibilities of a people. Narratives thereby serve as cultural paradigms, organizing a community's experiences around a common repertoire of widely known personae and drama. Stanley Hauerwas observes that "stories suggest how we should see and describe the world—that is how we should 'look-on' our selves, others, and the world—in ways that rules taken in themselves do not." As a result, our "character is constituted by the . . . stories that are combined to give a design or unity to the variety of things we must and must not do in our lives."[21] Drama critic Martin Esslin extends this perspective to television:

> Though it may well be true that our present-day archetypal heroes cut pale figures when set side by side with those of earlier cultures, the genesis of today's archetypes is by no means as different as it might appear at first glance. . . . The pantheon of archetypal characters in ever-recurring situations on present-day American television does, I believe, accurately reflect the collective psyche, the collective fears and aspirations, neuroses and nightmares of the average American, as distinct from the factual reality of the state of the nation. Does not the prominence of hospitals and disease in story lines indicate a national preoccupation with health, even a certain hypochondria? Do not the sex kittens of the evening series actually represent current ideals of beauty? Are not the mix-ups and grotesqueries of family situation comedies an accurate, if exaggerated, scenario of the embarrassments and triumphs of family life, real or fantasized? . . . These then are the collective daydreams of this culture.[22]

Television drama today has such a mythopoetic character. It creates and enacts stories not merely to entertain but to help us locate our individual lives in the broader drama of the culture. Producers of television drama, who have the most control in the artistic and economic processes of creating shows, are acolytes in the liturgies taking place every evening on the network stage. These acolytes wield significant cultural power as they project fictional worlds with real-life consequences. Yet their authority, like that of a priest, must always be granted by the faithful followers. If their narratives are at odds with what the parishioners wish to believe, the televised church runs the risk of losing its congregation; the audience turns off the set or even abandons the medium. Over the years this has been proved most clearly in the lack of tragedy on American television. The congregation of viewers hopes that life will end happily for all of those who are not terribly evil, and they will not watch most narratives that suggest otherwise.

The more "mass" the medium, the more general the mythopoetic expression of the medium's popular stories. Because television is probably the most popular storyteller of American society, its myths are very broadly conceived and rarely anchored in the particular religious beliefs or ethnic and racial experiences of specific social groups. Often popular stories appear to be produced by no one in particular for everyone in general.[23] Even so, they are worthy of our careful interpretation and critique; there may be no better route to a religiously transparent appraisal of modern culture, where no one appears to believe anything in particular and everyone seems to follow the same popular narratives.

## Exegesis of Television Narratives

Television appears to be the major storyteller of our age. Certainly television has a large audience in the United States, every evening attracting roughly 60 percent of the nation's households. Adults in some Western nations today see more drama on the tube in one year than pretelevision generations viewed on the stage or screen in a lifetime. Nearly everyone recognizes the medium's major artifacts (e.g., "Dallas") and celebrities (e.g., Johnny Carson), and many people follow closely the escapades of their favorite personae. Television's dramatic structures and formulas are mimicked by children and mocked by satirists. On college campuses — even in faculty dining areas — television programs are regularly a resource for conversation and discussion.

The most important questions about the role of popular storytelling in human life cannot be adequately answered through quantitative studies. Imagine reducing the issue of television violence to the results of experiments or surveys; however, this is done every year by consumer groups, religious organizations, and government-supported researchers in the United States. Such research overlooks some of the most fundamental features of storytelling used for centuries to examine and interpret the significance of narrative in culture: the difference between portrayal and point of view, the reflective nature of storytelling and story listening, the phenomenon of vicarious participation, and especially the mythopoetic aspects of public narrative.

*complexity of analyzing the use of narrative...*

Popular narrative such as television drama can serve a mythic function especially in mass societies where indigenous folk narrative is not experienced communally by all people. In such situations popular tales told on television may create a web of common public belief which transcends ethnic and religious variations among the populace. Through easily apprehended characters, settings, and plots, popular storytellers project meaningful, widely experienced fictional worlds that become part of the symbolic universe inhabited by the society. John Narone writes, "The attitudes and images, the symbols and metaphors of the myth, disclose the character of the individual's hopes, the quality of his dreams."[24] Other media, such as newspapers, radio, and magazines, reinforce the role of these narratives by discussing and describing them, relating them to other areas of life, and expanding the contexts of experience.

Because television drama often functions in society as religious narrative functions in religious communities, we ought to interpret television drama as a sacred text for the culture viewing it. This is not to imply that all narratives are equal in their consequences for society or that narratives promulgated by a religious community function precisely the same as popular stories. For most people, reading the Bible is not the same type of experience as watching television, although the various types of televangelism based on "secular" program formats blur the traditional distinctions between religious and nonreligious television. Nor are all myths disseminated through narrative epistemologically equal; the veracity of a narrative is independent of this argument, although it is an essential issue for any television researcher or critic. Rather, the point is that both popular and religious narratives, especially in advanced industrial societies, help locate the individual in a meaningful world. As Sallie TeSelle writes, "We learn who we are through the stories we embrace as our own—the story of my life is structured by the larger stories (social, political, mythic) in which I understand my personal story to take place."[25] Television is one of those mythic narratives, competing with others, including those offered by religious communities. Televised stories may not always be the strongest sources of narrative meaning in a particular culture or for specific individuals, but neither is religious narrative. Contemporary humankind can choose among numerous storytelling sources. At least in the case of commercial television, we know that a majority of the public follows its narratives.

By approaching television drama as a significant source of narrative in society, we may interpret television as the anthropologist investigates cultural artifacts or as the religious scholar explains a text. Although his point is a bit overstated, Tom Diver argues similarly for print narratives that "theology is to religious narrative as literary criticism is to literature."[26] Story invariably animates culture, and a critical exegesis of the major storytellers of contemporary society yields an understanding of some of that society's fundamental beliefs and values. Arguing the hermeneutical analogy for popular art, we might call the interpretation of television "lower criticism with a higher purpose."

Stretching the analogy, such television criticism should

be patterned after biblical interpretation. We gain an understanding of a culture by appealing to its sacred narratives, locating the significant context for those stories, and examining how the narratives and the people define each other. More specifically, we move from an examination of the text (the program, series, or genre), to an elucidation of its context (the cultural and historical setting of the people for whom the program is meaningful, as well the material conditions of its creation and financing), and finally to the application (the informed meaning of the text for humankind today).

In the case of television drama, the text is not a script but a performance of a narrative. Because television packages almost everything as a story, television narrative takes many different forms, from commercials to news and talk shows. The performance is the result of the work of many people, including writers, directors, performers, technicians, and especially producers.[27] Each influences the resulting dramatic production. However, there is no simple way to explain the content of television drama merely as a reflection of the values of the people who make it, as some have tried.[28] Popular narrative is usually produced within a creative paradigm that, like scientific paradigms, indicates the rules of the game. Those rules, in turn, are established over years as various programs succeed or fail in the audience ratings. Artistic control over most television drama is so widely dispersed among program makers and distributors (primarily the commercial networks) that in the end audience ratings drive the system of production. New television programs are derived largely from particular narrative formulations that have proved to be successful in the recent past (e.g., "Dallas," "Hill Street Blues," and the "Cosby Show" soon begat imitations). In this sense the producer is the acolyte, serving the worshipping congregation as well as the priests of high finance.

The "soul" of a television drama, to use Aristotle's phrase from *Poetics,* is the plot. Plot relates the various elements of the story to each other, resulting in a myth rather than a mere chronicle of events. These plot formulas largely identify the type of television program and even dictate the kinds of characters who are likely to appear in the story. In the case of the daytime soap opera, for example, the lack of a central plot and the proliferation of various subplots give the genre its form and meaning. Changes in characterization, setting, costuming, and even language are important as well, since they too probably reflect and influence culture. However, it is the way popular narrative embraces various plot formulas, and secondarily the way it casts major characters, that should most concern the scholar who wishes to interpret the mythic dimensions of television. As Kort suggests, the plot more than anything else gives narrative its coherence.[29]

## The Television Critic as Exegete

A growing community of television scholars agrees that television drama merits serious interpretation even though it might not always elicit deep aesthetic appreciation.[30] Although they might not like the exegetical analogy, these television scholars would agree that criticism ought to deal with text, context, and application. However, there would be tremendous disagreement about the meaning of "application" in the act of criticism. The Marxist and the structuralist, for example, would likely raise widely different issues and offer opposing criticism.

As a critical act, application permits the critic to clarify her presuppositions and to engage directly in explicitly nonscientific discussion with both scholars and the public. The critic should address directly the concerns of people throughout the ages — love, virtue, justice, and peace — using television to address contemporary manifestations of these concerns, such as nationalism, militarization, materialism, authoritarianism, sexism, spiritual rebellion, and moral decadence. After all, the purpose is not merely to understand or evaluate television but to participate in the public discussion about society and culture. Criticism is not for the sake of criticism any more than scholarship should be for the sake of scholarship but is instead an ongoing dialogue with the industry which produces the narratives and the culture which enjoys them.

To put it differently, the television critic works with one interpretive foot in the culture and the other in her own narrative as researcher. She not only explains the significance of a televised story but reveals the implications of the story from her own perspective. She stands like an Old Testament prophet, evaluating the culture of Baal from the vantage point of her own academically sacred traditions. Television interpretation, then, is necessarily the clash of narratives, one the story of the program (and the culture in which it is popular) and the other the biography of the critic (and the academic community). The critic presupposes the veracity of her own narrative in order to interpret and evaluate the beliefs that animate the broader culture.

The issue of "objectivity," at least as it is frequently invoked by social scientists, is of little concern in this endeavor. Rather than seeking to eliminate the "bias" of the researcher, criticism should reveal the presuppositions of the researcher. As Walter Fisher has argued, standard social-scientific theories of human communication either "ignore the role of values or they deny the possibility of developing rational schemes for their assessment. They thereby disregard ultimate questions of good and evil."[31] The Baconian epistemology of the social sciences is more concerned with predictability and power than with understanding and evaluation. Although analytic and postanalytic philosophers (other than Alasdair MacIntyre) have generally neglected the idea of narrative, it is compatible with all but the most rigid foundationalism. Since the interpretation of a public narrative must first be grounded in the text and context, any kind of simplistic moralizing, ideological raving, or religious proselytizing is likely to be obvious. A critique of a popular narrative ought to frame the story in the critic's own perspective openly. It is impossible to eliminate the moral, ideological, or religious perspectives in criticism. The worst kind of criticism pretends that presuppositions are unimportant or do not exist. According to Julian Hartt, this kind of thinking has caused the "mantle of the prophets" to descend upon "secular shoulders."[32]

## Genre as Liturgy

The fact that two television scholars will sometimes offer contradictory interpretations and evaluations of the same program reveals the subjective nature of criticism. But subjectivity
should not discourage the critic or researcher, for ambiguity and
ideology are inescapably part of social investigation. As Louis
Wirth wrote fifty years ago:

> The scientific study of social phenomena is not yet institution-
> alized like the study of physical and biological phenomena.
> The student of society will be plagued by the difficulties of
> achieving "objectivity," by the existence of social values, by
> the competition with common-sense knowledge, by the limits
> of his freedom and capacity to experiment, and by other seri-
> ous and peculiar handicaps which trouble the natural scientist
> less or not at all. But the social scientist, whose very subject
> matter is the social world, can avoid studying the processes
> and problems of man in society only by pretending to be
> something he is not, or by lapsing into such a remote degree
> of abstraction or triviality as to make the resemblance be-
> tween what he does and what he professes to be doing purely
> coincidental.[33]

Much of the difficulty in studying television programming, however, is made tolerable by the formulaic nature of popular programming. Like most art through the ages, today's television shows rely on well-known themes and structures derived
largely from earlier dramatic forms, from classical theater to
vaudeville. As Newcomb points out in his essay in this volume, few
producers or writers have the freedom to reinvent the dramatic
wheel; they inherit past ways of thinking about and making programs as well as various institutional constraints that encourage
them to imitate previously successful art forms. The situation comedy and the soap opera, for example, have remained the same as
much as they have changed since the early years of American television. Artists imitate and audiences expect such imitation, as they
always have. Television is ritual.

Secular television programming shares with religious worship the necessity of public ritual. Both a church service and a television program require prescribed forms of ritual before "participation" is really possible. One could not enjoy or understand a completely innovative show any more than one could really worship a completely unknown god in a foreign church service. Like the mass, television is structured in prescribed ways so that the worshippers may enter into meaningful communion. Television uses its own liturgies to ensure communal experience.

On the tube the various liturgies are embodied in the traditional dramatic genres. There are situation comedies, westerns, detective shows, soap operas, ensemble programs, and action shows. Various liturgical hybrids appear occasionally, but by and large the genres survive as distinct formulas for organizing plots, establishing characters, and introducing settings. Some programs even return to their formulaic roots after venturing into new variations. In many respects the "Cosby Show" is more akin to the optimistic and predictable domestic comedies of the 1950s and early 1960s, such as "Leave It to Beaver" and "My Three Sons," than to the cynical and satirical programs of the 1970s, such as "All in the Family" and "M*A*S*H." The religious dimensions of television programs are best examined in terms of both continuity and change in these genres.

Newcomb is certainly correct that it makes an enormous difference whether we examine individual programs, series, genres, or viewing patterns. The interpretive net must be thrown broadly to catch genres if one seeks to determine the mythic significance of television for a culture. Fundamental changes and shifts in genres highlight the significance of various programs, just as revisions in church liturgies and books of common prayer often reflect shifting conceptions of deity, truth, and religious practice. Consider, for example, the changing character of the television soap opera from its earliest versions in the 1950s to the present. Early ones centered on the lives of common heroines who were rewarded for their hard work, perseverance, and moral purity. This optimistic system of personal rewards was gradually replaced by an increasingly chaotic and unpredictable world of personal alienation and dramatic impotence. Many heroes disappeared; no characters could conquer evil and usher in permanent financial or romantic salvation. The highly popular evening serials, including "Dallas" and "Dynasty," are excellent examples from the last decade. Although they focus more on corporate conflict than the daytime soap operas do, the nighttime programs are likewise more morally ambiguous than the early soaps. There are fewer signs of salvation from evil in such shows, which resemble in a metaphorical sense existentialist drama, such as that of Samuel Beckett, where the characters are forever "waiting for Godot."

Changes in drama over the years should not blind us to the similarities and consistencies. The overall continuity in television mythopoetics over the decades is remarkable. American programming presents an amazingly coherent source of beliefs and hopes. As Newcomb puts it, modern popular television privileges redundancy and repetition over novelty. Again, to draw on the religious parallel, despite the differences among religious denominations and the shifts in liturgy and worship over the centuries, there is a significant continuity of faith between believers then and now.

By focusing on television genres, the television critic can avoid the temptation to claim too much about the social significance of a particular program. The biblical scholar faces the same problem when he attempts to interpret the state of early Jewish or Christian life on the basis of a single chapter of the sacred narratives. Indeed, even the Bible has its own genres, from the Old Testament wisdom literature to the New Testament epistles and synoptic Gospels. The exegete frequently learns about different aspects of the biblical story and derives different applications from the various parts of the canon. But such applications are most compelling when they are integrated into the broad sweep of biblical history painted by the entire story of redemptive history. Some television critics today are like fundamentalist preachers in that they use individual "proof texts" from particular program episodes to explain major social or cultural changes in America. This is dangerous scholarship, for it so easily condemns or lauds an entire industry based on a few products. The success of the "Cosby Show," for instance, was interpreted as evidence that black America had finally gained respect, even though the race of the Huxtables may have had little or nothing to do with the show's popularity. After all, Cosby had been a successful comedian and television personality for years, and the economic status and social standing of blacks in the United States had changed little in the years immediately preceding the program.

The overall shift in situation comedies from the 1970s to the 1980s deserves serious scrutiny. The optimistic spirit of the "Cosby Show" and other comedies of the 1980s was a relatively clear break from the cynicism and despair of the 1970s. Americans laughed along with the television in the 1970s, but such humor typically lacked the strong optimism of Cosby's show. Love triumphs for the Huxtables, whereas hypocrisy would continue for the Bunkers. The "Cosby Show" and the other optimistic sitcoms of the 1980s were like an act of contrition for the social sins and faithlessness of the previous decade. Americans simultaneously reelected President Ronald Reagan, who spoke of the nation as a special city on a hill, close to the heavens and predestined to play a part in the democratic salvation of the world. They also participated as television viewers in the ritual of proclaiming their faith by believing along with the show's characters that all things would work together for good in the end. In this sense the newer sitcoms proclaimed a secular version of the Pauline statement that all things would work together for good for those who love the Lord (Romans 8:28). During the same period "the family" became a focus of public discussion, and even the major news magazines and newspapers reported on the apparent strength of the traditional family structure amid a variety of challenges from the "new morality."

## Television as Prophet

There are two kinds of prophets in the world: those who speak what people wish to hear and those who claim to speak the unpopular truth. The former are given their authority by the people, who seek to have their desires confirmed by a prophetic voice. The latter receive their authority from a special revelation, presumably direct from the Almighty. Television is given its prophetic authority by the congregation of faithful viewers, which expresses its approval in audience ratings. Since the advent of television drama four decades ago, the tube has been an American prophet, formulating and reformulating at least three widely believed myths.

**MYTH 1: GOOD WILL TRIUMPH OVER EVIL.** No myth has been chanted more on television. Across the genres, and through the various changes in programming over the years, regular television programming has largely stayed clear of tragedy and unhappy endings of all types. From sitcom to western and detective program, viewers have been treated repeatedly to the victories of good over evil. Throughout the centuries religious faith has typically included the most fundamental belief that virtuous actions of humans or deities would usher in salvation. Often the salvation was freedom from the bondage of sin, oppression, or injustice. In southern black experience it was the sweet chariot which eventually would overcome the misery and grief of slavery. For the Jews it was oppression by the Egyptians. Whatever the society, humankind has felt the need for reassurance that all things would work together for good in the end. Today television dramas assure Americans daily that the forces of good, whether in the form of the detective or the loving sitcom parent, will be the victors in the battle against evil. Family problems are worked out and criminals are brought to justice. Peace and harmony are possible to those who keep the faith.

Even in the soap opera, the modern champion of the serial form, the viewer is driven to the set with expectation of an end. Only because the contemporary viewer believes in the myth of good triumphing over evil are "unending" stories part of the stock of the television trade. Newcomb points out that this type of television challenges the Aristotelian assumption that stories must have an ending for them to be drama. However, his focus on the serial is overstated for three reasons: (1) the vast majority of programming is not in serial form, (2) much of the serial programming, such as the evening ensemble shows like "Hill Street Blues" and "L.A. Law," contain subplots which indeed come to a close, and (3) viewers expect closure in the programs. Even the action in serials appears to be driven toward a significant conclusion which has not yet been written but which will come to pass. There is hope.

**MYTH 2: EVIL EXISTS ONLY IN THE HEARTS OF A FEW EVIL PEOPLE.** Good will triumph over evil in large measure because people are basically good. Evil is not a spiritual force beyond human control, as depicted in the Devil or Satan. Nor is evil somehow part of the human condition, residing in the soul of all people. Instead, television mythology limits evil to the condition that wicked people find themselves in, whether by poor upbringing, association with a bad crowd, or personal rebelliousness.

Television emphasizes this personal side of evil almost to the exclusion of institutional evil. Because only individuals are bad, not corporations or nations, for instance, evil is easily checked as hoods are thrown in jail and villains of all kinds are brought to justice. Sin can be corralled, whether by the police or the cavalry, so that good people can go on living the good life that was intended for them. Even the most cynical and despairing programs on television during the turbulent 1970s, such as "M*A*S*H" and "All in the Family," could not end on a purely tragic basis.

By objectifying evil in the actions and bodies of particular evil characters, television reaffirms the hope that wickedness and immorality of all types can be kept under human control. Humankind can be delivered from evil. Unexpected and unlucky events occur, but in the end the potential evil consequences are kept from escalating beyond the grasp of humankind.

**MYTH 3: GODLINESS EXISTS IN THE GOOD AND EFFECTIVE ACTIONS OF INDIVIDUALS.** Only on rare occasions and programs has television even hinted at the existence of an omnipotent or omniscient deity. Instead, the tube has traded the mysterious and unexplainable for a more humanly understandable conception of God: virtuous and effective human action.

In other words, the god of American television is found in humanistic pragmatism. Humankind's ability to ensure its own survival and usher in progress is not delivered from heaven but is the result of the efficacious actions of individual people. These are the saints of prime-time television, solving crimes, reconciling love-lost couples, and clearing up confusion and complication. The father of a sitcom and the captain of the police force make a difference in the world by rescuing innocent victims and helping others put their lives back together. The gospel according to television is clear: have faith in individuals.

Significantly absent from nearly all television drama are the cardinal virtues. Television saints accomplish much good, but rarely because of prudence, temperance, or fortitude. Television even reduces justice, one of the most significant virtues throughout the history of Western civilization, to the revengeful triumph of good guys over bad guys. In other words, the right conduct of television heroes is rarely set in the context of ethical reasoning or virtuous action. Instead, it is simply the efficacious works of a pragmatic person committed to success. Television prophesies the remuneration of individual achievement; it has little time for virtue.

## Television as Religion

Throughout the history of broadcasting, scholars of the media have distinguished between religious and secular programming. In a narrow sense such a simple typology was valuable; some broadcasts are more obviously religious in style and substance. Church services and revivalistic programs, such as those of Jimmy Swaggart and Billy Graham, are unquestionably "religious." Even some of the more recent programs, such as the talk show format of the "700 Club," are clearly centered around religious discussion and entertainment.

From a broader perspective, however, it is not so clear that only ostensibly religious broadcasts are religious. Only if we restrict "religion" to the beliefs and practices of the institutional church can we legitimately claim that most television drama is not religious. In the institutional church, the substance of faith is expressed primarily through the broad themes of the sacred Scriptures: Creation, Fall, Redemption, Second Coming. In television, too, the basic tenets are broadly thematic, held together by the ways that program genres integrate plot, character, and setting. No single television series, or worse yet a particular episode, constitutes the corpus of popular religious belief today. Rather, just as the beliefs of the faithful churchgoers are not always made explicit in a particular sermon or in one season of worship, the faith of television viewers is evident only in the broad sweep of televised narrative.

Television's religiosity is granted by the viewers and the producers, who have turned the medium into one of the major storytellers of American society. Narratives on the tube tell us what we wish to believe, inviting our participation in the story of popular religion. In the end, we support this televised religion. We grant the programmers a privileged role in culture as prophets. We send the messages to the advertisers as to which narratives we will embrace as our own. Unlike the real church, which claims its authority from on high, the televised church derives its power from the congregation. Television drama today is religion in its most popular and secular forms. Like those commercials unearthed in the dusty vault beneath "Fun City," it narrates our own story of American civilization.

## Religion on Television

### HORACE M. NEWCOMB

𝕴 will not survey the presentation or representation of religion in television fiction. Such a survey is impossible. The vast text, what Nick Browne calls the "megatext," of television history is not available for survey, nor is one memory a sufficient source.[1] Nevertheless, I do wish to cite concrete examples wherever possible, realizing that countless counterexamples exist in each viewer's experience.

Moreover, these counterexamples are rooted in the religious as well as televisual experiences of viewers. What counts for religion on television is as much a theological issue as it is an issue grounded in textual or narrative theory, in theories of communication and culture, or in theories of ideology and media. One person's religious television is another's secular mess.

Let me begin, then, by setting out my own understanding of the television megatext. I agree with Schultze (see chap. 1 of this volume) that the only real way to understand religion on television is through an examination of the great sweep of the medium, its very bulk. I also agree that there are enormous religious implications in the forms of television as well as in the content of particular programs. But the organization of the megatext may work in a somewhat different manner than either Browne or Schultze suggests.

## Similarity and Difference

The key point of difference, not merely with those writers but with any number of commentators on television, has to do with a fundamental way of looking at this medium, or at any aspect of cultural expression that results in a large amount of similar material. One must decide to look at the relation and ratio between similarity and difference. As simple as this sounds, it becomes a crucial critical and analytical factor when considering the popular and folk expressions that depend on repetition, redundancy, pattern, formula, and, what is most central to television, seriality. Thus, an analysis of quilts or folk songs or westerns will differ depending on whether the analyst chooses to concentrate on how each instance varies and alters given patterns or to concentrate on how each instance confirms the patterns.

In the contemporary, industrialized, mass-mediated forms of popular culture we can best begin a discussion with the notion of "regulated difference," which allows us to recognize the necessity of change, the power of audiences to influence content, the role of producers as cultural interpreters, and so on. Here again, if we concentrate on "regulation," we will most likely engage in ideological analysis, showing how structures of economics and the hegemonic forces inherent in any social formation control difference for special interests. If we concentrate on "difference," we will show how gaps appear in the apparently seamless ideological fabric.

In the case of religion, one might argue that producers attempt to appeal to varied audiences by showing slightly different aspects of religious life, or that they might capitalize on current events to appeal to audiences attuned to television's role as the great presenter of those events. Or one could argue that whatever aspects of religion appear on television are carefully contained within larger structures. In fact, the last seems to be more the case. The most common religious references on television follow patterns developed earlier in film, radio, and popular fiction, which used to be the major storytellers for the culture. In a recent discussion with the producers of "Magnum, P.I.," I suggested a story line in which the detective would be hired to protect a television evangelist who had come to Hawaii to rest and recuperate after a scandal that resulted in threats on his life. The story would have the two men become friends, as the detective learned that the preacher was not as bad as he had expected, whatever "bad" might mean under the circumstances of the story. The two men would also discover common ground in Vietnam War experiences, drawing on the old "no atheists in foxholes" motif, and the preacher would exhibit a violent streak when he and the detective were attacked — by his own supporters, it would turn out, who were after the cash involved in the big-business aspects of his enterprises. Magnum would keep him from killing someone. The preacher would acknowledge the violent aspects of his character, confess that in controlling it he had to have God's help, say that this is why he tries to lead others to salvation, and go home chastened by all his experiences, but more committed than ever to his calling.

I thought it was a good story, but the producers were less thrilled. The telling moment came when one simply said something like, "And you know, religion is so hard to deal with. You're always going to offend someone. We just try to stay away. . . ."

Of *course* I knew this. I was pitching a little difference at the regulated, and in this case at the regulators and the implied regulations. I was pitching it because I think of this show as innovative, at times daringly experimental. I was pitching it because I thought it completely in keeping with the character and the fictional world of the series (particularly in light of later stories to which I'll return) and because I thought we could keep well within the bounds of taste and convention while stretching audience perceptions a bit. We could reveal a familiar character as unfamiliar, and I refer both to the stock formulaic character of "media evangelist" *and* to the personally familiar character of Magnum.

This example indicates why this question of similarity and difference is so important. It reminds us that we have fallen back on the use of similarity in the study of popular forms for two reasons. The first is simple. In dealing with the bulk of mass media, it is easier to organize critical analysis around studies of form and formula, genre and structure, repetition and sameness. This is a purely functional choice. The second reason for focusing on similarity is far more complex. It is partially expressed by Schultze as well as by others who suggest that *meaning* resides in those formal familiarities. Whether we discuss formulas, genres, patterns, or, in this context, rituals, we are discussing meaningful structures, the *content* that is to be found in structural analyses of all sorts.

The latest potent version of this approach is found in the negative version of postmodernism, best expressed recently in the Gitlin anthology *Watching Television*.[2] Here all difference is merely surface glitter, or perhaps clutter. All that counts is that everything is washed into similarity, that the most serious and the most meretricious of issues are jammed against one another in a meaningless mix of image and flow. Thus, all detective shows are the same. All comedies are the same. The sameness is what matters.

Well it does and it doesn't. We must take care to understand this medium in its particularities as well as in its generalities. For this reason I have suggested the utility of examining the dialogic aspects of the medium, the particular voices, messages, and meanings embedded within the similarity.[3] Indeed, because this accounts for television's power and appeal to multiple audiences, we must conceive of television texts in more particular ways that relate to actual viewing experience. Like Fiske's concept of semiotic excess, this perspective relies upon recent audience studies demonstrating the vast range of viewing strategies that are rooted in specific social contexts.[4]

The point is that we might come to different conclusions by using varying notions of the actual text of television. I agree completely with Schultze when he suggests that story is central to television, to religion, and to life. But a great deal depends on whether we look at individual programs, at series, at genres, at the schedule, or at evenings of television that viewers experience. Only with careful distinction will we be able to regulate and monitor the relations among structure, form, and content and among various theological positions that might frame religious meaning in different ways. Certainly for purposes of analysis and for the experiences of viewers, it makes a difference whether we find religious meaning in the social, cultural, and ideological structures regulating television, in the unique forms of its narrative strategies, or in the content of specific stories.

To see these things best we must turn to specific examples of television programming. We are all familiar with the widely shared level of popular cultural expressions of religious attitude. We know how to react when we hear the familiar phrases such as "the man upstairs" or "the big guy," usually uttered with a shrug or a roll of the eyes. We recognize teary-eyed moments of self-sacrifice. Within this context we have a specific set of religious signifiers: Jewish guilt and humor, often related to an individual's youthful religious experiences; the Roman collar as an acceptable signifier of religion, church, piety; the southern evangelical, Protestant in some nonspecific way, sometimes black; the Hindu guru, almost always pathetically distracted and comic; the generalized religious "psychotic," zealous, often violent, sexually confused and repressed, and so on.

These aspects of religion are considered safe, neutral, and are often used because of their immediate visual qualities. They are part of television's narrative shorthand and represent received, confirmed aspects of religious life. Their very "sameness," rather than any meaningful "difference," makes them useful not only to producers but to audiences. We can criticize and question the substitution of these stereotypes for the rich variety of actual religious experience and for a deeper sense of religious life. We cannot, of course, completely deny their existence, indeed their powerful sources, in actual experience. Recent events surrounding the PTL scandal, for example, exceed any imaginative creation of the most blatant representation of religious charlatanism.

Yet even these shorthand devices take on special significance in the context of individual programs. They come into play, they function, they stand out differently, in varied settings. Here is an example from the pilot episode of the series, "J. J. Starbuck." This series, starring old television hand Dale Robertson, focused on a Texas billionaire (a rapidly disappearing breed, which might have made the show more or less interesting) who traveled the country in a Cadillac, monitoring his investments and solving mysteries. It mixed down-home homily with folklike "sayings." It presented Starbuck as a bearer of strong traditional values, painting him as a sort of sympathetic, sometimes self-effacing, very rich "good Samaritan." In this episode he helps a very young man trap an evil stepfather, the murderer of the boy's mother. In the process he becomes the boy's legal guardian, teaches him that raw vengeance is bad, and solves a number of personal problems for other characters.

In the very last scene of the show, as Starbuck and the boy drive away, the old man is heard in voice-over. At one point he says, "The value of anything is determined by the amount of human life expended for it." I found this sentence peculiarly religious. It wasn't very specific, but it was a strong assertion. It made me question whether I would agree. It resonated of Jewish and Christian scriptures, of Buddhist sacrifice and self-immolation, of holy wars of all sorts. Its emphasis on the human could easily lend credence to charges of secular humanism, but such charges would demonstrate the often facile thinking of supporters of that perspective.

That the comment was embedded in an otherwise innocuous context is directly to the point here. Religion on television is often part of the generalized cultural fabric presented in this, the central story system of our time. The question remains, however, as to whether such generalizations rob the religious of any significance, or whether they place religion in the service of corrupt values.

A second example is perhaps even more indicative of this threaded, woven nature of religion. It came near the end of the first episode of the medical drama, "Buck James." Patterned on a real-life trauma surgeon, Dr. Red Duke, Buck James played a Houston doctor equally at home on the range or the emergency ward floors. In this episode he faced a number of personal and professional problems. One of them placed him in the role of physical hero, saving a trapped construction worker from the high beams of a building in progress. We followed Buck as he made his way through his plot, returning several times to the construction worker to monitor progress. In the end it's clear to all concerned, including the patient, that he's about to die. As Buck leans over him, the weakened man says something like, "You know, it ain't so bad." Buck replies, "No, it ain't so bad. Everybody's got to do it. You're just going on ahead of the rest of us."

Again, there's not much specificity here. No specific doctrine. No dogma. But the moment was dramatically powerful, calling up death scenes, the problems of facing and defining death, notions of how to die, of immortality and afterlife, of how to comfort, even of how to make claims about death. Death was put not in a general statement but in a specific one. It could have *seemed* somewhat general, somewhat like the stereotypical "man upstairs" lines, and certainly it echoed generalized, familiar sentiments. But within the texture of character, drama, and even genre, it demonstrated that a return to the familiar, to the similar, is not always a failure to deal with the specificity of issues. Constantly to privilege the innovative in expressive culture misses the sense in which the central expressive forms of any society have a legitimate purpose in conserving, repeating, and restating.

A third example throws a slightly different shadow on this discussion. Here again, the most overt religious moment occurs at the dramatic climax of the television episode. Again, it is very familiar, bordering on the stereotypical and the cliché. A self-centered and weak brother, a prize-fight promoter, has used his good-hearted younger sibling to feather his own nest. The younger man is a prize fighter, not very good, and his task is to lose fights so a mobster can make money. The older brother is supposed to make money, too, but he's so far into gambling debt that he can't find his way out. The younger brother simply accepts his lot, knowing that someday they will climb up and he will be allowed to show his real stuff.

Enter another promising young fighter and his sister. The younger brother teaches the new fighter some tricks that make him quite good, and he also falls in love with the sister. At the end, the story is quite predictable. The two young men are supposed to fight. The brother doesn't want to throw this one. He tries to fight and is beaten up. But the fact that he won't fall down means that the gangsters are out to get him and his brother. As they're about to kill the older brother, a trainer, a relatively minor character, steps into the ring with him.

You have to protect your younger brother, he tells the promoter. You have a "friend" who's "bigger than you" who will help. When a thug moves in, the trainer throws him across the ring with a mighty toss. Another thug pulls a gun and fires at the trainer. But the trainer dodges, and when he opens his hands, he shows everyone, including us, that he has *caught the bullets.* Terrified, the thugs flee, the brothers unite, the lovers renew their pledges, and off we go.

This is an unfair example for the argument I'm trying to make. It's unfair because it is so blatant and because I hardly knew the series from which it came, "Highway to Heaven," one of the few overtly religious programs on television. I suspect that the episode was atypical. Ordinarily, I think, Michael Landon (here playing the supernatural boxing trainer) went about wielding his angelic power in more gentle, less specifically wondrous ways. I believe he convinced, persuaded, led people to experience their better selves in much the same manner as he did in "Little House on the Prairie." Still, there is little question that his supernatural acts, as reminiscent of "Superman" as they were, expressed religious sentiments for some viewers, especially in the setting of this program.

Two more examples fall somewhere between generalized but potentially powerful notions of widely shared values and stupidly spectacular attempts at the supernatural—bullet-catching angels, indeed. Both "St. Elsewhere" and "Magnum, P.I." have, in recent years, tried to represent "out-of-body" experiences. Both were couched in strongly spiritual terms. Both had powerful consequences for the characters involved. And we might speculate that both had consequences for viewers as well, not necessarily in any specific, behavioral sense, but certainly in terms of how the characters and the series could be viewed following such story lines.

In "St. Elsewhere" Wayne Fiscus, comic hot-wire of the emergency room, is shot while on duty. As friends work feverishly on his body, and later operate extensively, Fiscus goes to heaven. At least he goes somewhere and there are plenty of skewed visuals. This becomes one of the nicest aspects of the program as we are presented with a thoughtful attempt to use camera and art direction in a way that suggests transcendence of normal perception. While in this setting Fiscus renews contacts with old friends and enemies and, in perhaps the most daring moment of the narrative, meets God.

God is represented by Fiscus himself, by the same actor talking to himself. Think about it for a moment, not as a trick, but as a theological statement. How *does* one represent the deity, particularly in a tradition in which such representation is almost always considered idolatrous? How does one even talk *about* God, much less create dialogue *for* God? At any rate, in this particular episode, Fiscus doesn't want to come back. But he's saved by the (God-given?) skills of his colleagues, is pulled back through the proverbial tunnel of light, and forced to become alive (himself?) again. The experience gave him new insight into his life and was referred to in subsequent episodes.

Magnum's experience was somewhat different. Designed to be the conclusion of the series, this episode also begins with the protagonist being shot. We then see Magnum walking up the beach to encounter his friend Mac, who was killed in an earlier episode. This is somewhat confusing, however, because regular viewers knew that another character, an exact double for Mac (and played by the same actor), appeared in a number of episodes. Magnum calls this new character "Mac" because he cannot escape the resemblance. Add to this the fact that the original Mac was killed in a car bombing designed for Magnum, and the character relationships become increasingly complex. In this episode, entitled "Limbo," we soon realize that Magnum is talking to the "spirit" of his dead friend. Mac has been sent to ease him into the afterlife.

Instead of going to heaven, however, as does Fiscus, Magnum remains in this world, but not of it. He can see and hear his friends and be present with them, but they have no knowledge of his presence. He "talks" to them, but they do not hear. Indeed, instead of an exploration of the formal nature of the afterlife and its eternal inhabitants, we have here a device through which the character relations of this *present* world are explored. People tell stories about Magnum much as people do in real life in similar circumstances. They also reassess their relations to him, evaluate their characters and his own, and genuinely explore the nature of intimate human interaction. We later learn that Magnum is lying in a coma, and in the opening episodes of the next season he came back to consciousness and fully recovered from his wounds.

Such a plot is not so farfetched in this series, which often explored various spiritual aspects of human experience. There have been instances of psychic or intuitive responses on the part of several characters, including Magnum. And in one episode when a friend lay in a coma of his own, Magnum suggested praying for him. When questioned about his belief in prayer, Magnum responded that he believed that one should pray to God, and then *act* as if there were no God. It's not a bad piece of theology, nor is it terribly removed from Fiscus experiencing himself as God.

## Immanence and Transcendence

All these examples—plus many others that any regular television viewer could add—indicate that there are many ways in which whatever we know as "religion" gets into television. This sort of generalized sense of some transcendental element of experience has not gone unnoticed. Recently, for example, Father Andrew Greeley took the lead article in a Sunday *New York Times* Arts and Leisure section to argue that situation comedy is our contemporary morality play.

The shows rarely draw explicit moral conclusions for us. Usually they do not insist on hammering home ethical principles. Rather they hint lightly at the skills and traits that sustain love.

A modern version of the medieval morality play has slipped into prime-time television almost without anyone noticing it.[5]

It is significant that Greeley, no mean morality-player himself, argues so strongly that television is a purveyor of religious values. His article cites a number of comedies that offer up lessons in love as exemplary projections of another Love, one that exceeds our normal expressions.

Not every critic would be satisfied to leave it at that, at "little morality plays." Clifford Christians, for example, argues that such soft, impressionistic representations do no more than reassert the centrality of humanity, of what he calls, after Sorokin, "sensate culture." Acknowledging the sort of content I have referred to and the sort that Greeley finds impressive, Christians argues that "all such pointings are metaphors about man only; they do not establish the transcendent dimension as a category on its own terms with unique configurations."

The "self-transcendent" cinematic type emphasizes that man cannot live without grace and universals and faith. In Kierkegaardian fashion, necessary leaps are accentuated, yet they are always leaps into the dark at best. In stressing that we can overcome meaninglessness from within ourselves . . . these programs assume *de facto* that sickness and cure have the same spawning bed.[6]

By contrast, Christians calls for overt, symbolic representation of the transcendent sphere of life and experience. He cites Paul Schrader's study of Ozu, Bresson, and Dreyer, *Transcendental Style in Film,* as his touchstone.[7] According to Schrader these directors establish a strong sense of reality, then introduce "a disparity, a hint that such realism does not fulfill," and then nudge us "toward the invisible viewed through the visible itself. A world which cannot be fitted into ordinary patterns of explanation."[8] Examples of these nudging symbols occupy brief moments in the films of the directors.

As I suggested earlier, it is on such grounds that the charges for secular humanism can be created and countered. But it should also be clear that there are two sorts of argument being constructed. The first is aesthetic and suggests that only certain sorts of forms and symbols can stand as hints of transcendence. Such a debate can never be resolved within the limits of impressionistic formalist criticism. Consider, for instance, a counterexample from Greeley's perspective. He cites sociologist Albert Bergesen's description of the "Cosby Show": "Family love is one of the tiny windows through which the Good or the Possible or God, if you want to use the term, peeks at us. It is in the little things of life, isn't it, that we often find the meaning of the big things."[9] Again, the equation of "God" with "the Good" or "the Possible" falls prey to charges of humanism and perhaps counters the notion that these "tiny windows" open toward a truly distinct, transcendent sphere of human experience. Still, it is more accurate to say that they do not point toward a transcendence that is narrowly, specifically, or denominationally defined. Particular viewers may yet find their transcendent symbols in varying places.

This view is reinforced when we realize that television pushes these symbols at us not from one side alone but from many. If it is a specific example of the transcendent we desire, we need look only to an early episode of "Hill Street Blues." There Frank Furillo leaves his office, having freed a man he knows to be guilty, freed him precisely so that he will be at the mercy of a killing mob. He drives through the dark night of his urban environment, parks his car, and enters an empty building. Only when the window of the confessional booth is drawn back and he utters the first request for confession do we realize that he has gone into church to confront the dark night of his soul. There is no question as to the distinction of this other world or of its "intrusion" into Furillo's sense of the ordinary. But there is another sense in which we put together ethnicity, small actions, daily life, codes of strict behavior, his alcoholism, and so on, and discover that this "otherness" is much at the ground of his being. And is this not central to our experiences of religion? On the whole we are not, most of us, prone to direct experiences of that "otherness" even though it may inform our every action.

Thus, when Alex Keaton's (of "Family Ties") best friend dies in an automobile accident and Alex ends up seeking psychological counseling, it seems strange to hear, in the middle of the interview, "Do you believe in God, Alex?" The young man refuses to answer the question and the unseen counselor allows him to move ahead in his wandering, pained narrative. Much later in the hour, however, the psychologist repeats the question. This time Alex, beaten down to basics by his own memory and introspection, faces the issue. "That's what it all comes down to, isn't it?" He allows as how he does believe, but then his description—dolphins playing at sea, flowers, and so on—slips back toward the secular, the general, the sensate.

Push, pull. Shift and change. Perspectives alter. Producers avoid the specifics of belief, the words of faith, and concrete images of the transcendent like the plague. Such specificity could cost them audience. In the meantime, we are given the deeply, powerfully embedded notions of the good that must come from . . . somewhere.

In short, the difference between Greeley and Christians is essentially a theological debate rather than a debate over the representation of religion. The same is true, in a different comparison, of the arguments (taken in their general, unprogrammatic sense) between secular humanists and hard-core fundamentalists who skewer television at every turn. Immanence and transcendence, the poles of many great religions, have come soundly home in popular culture since the rise of the modern era. Peter Brooks argues in *The Melodramatic Imagination* that after the French Revolution killed off transcendence, melodrama took up our mighty symbols of good and evil and allowed us to live, and judge, with them.[10] And there is a sound position in Christian theology that immanence is as true a gospel as any. It behooves us, then, to clarify our theological positions as we carry out our critical analyses of the role of religion in mass culture, popular culture, or television. We can too easily assume that all that is immanent is in league with the dominant.

We can assume that the immanent is no more than the "priestly" function of religious value, while the truly "prophetic" demands the transcendental symbol. If these two are set out as polarities, we lose the sense and value of the priestly message, which often as not *is* profoundly implicated in the dominant culture. To put this in currently popular terms of cultural analysis, the sort of religious representation I have pointed out here would be no more than another hegemonic voice maintaining the status quo at the expense of real social change or, for that matter, of real religious provocation. In these terms, the real change would occur only with a religious representation that challenged all that. Greeley's praise of warm family love would be seen as no more than a powerful support for patriarchy. And searches for "self-understanding" caused by near death would be mere restatements of the comfortable political order.

There is much to favor in such an analysis, but I suggest two responses. First, and briefly, I think there is much in tradition, in the conventional order, in dominant ideology, in priestly voices, in hegemonic structures that should be maintained. All too often we use those terms as synonyms only for the negative aspects of the systems described. But there is more to any system than that.

Secondly, and finally, we can argue on aesthetic rather than theological grounds. Here we must return to the earlier notions of similarity and difference. The primary theological implication of television lies in its most fundamental structure as a form rooted in serial narrative. Whatever the material causes, the economic and sociological mechanisms that generate this narrative form, it is significant that for the first time in human experience, a mechanical form of expression takes on the character, not the illusion, of the human storyteller. Television, building on hints offered by radio, breaks the Aristotelian notion that stories must have a beginning, middle, and end. In television the stories never have to end.

Soap opera, of course, is the paradigm here. And the prime-time serial narratives of various sorts have accomplished much of their success on this formal distinction. But even in the most repetitive, redundant, and cyclical of episodic television, the long-term narrative stakes alter every instance of the story. Indeed, we don't *know* the real story of a television series until we experience it as a serial.

It is significant that within this serialization of narrative, within this form of storytelling that is now shared by more audiences than any other except oral storytelling, we have so much repetition. As Eco reminds us, the "valorization" of novelty is a rather new thing in the history of art. And the prevalence of television is, in his view, a move to a "truly post-post-modern" form of narration.[11] I prefer to cast this another way: Television is a return to a premodern form of storytelling in which novelty was not privileged over redundancy and repetition.

This suggests that our search for the prophetic voice, for the unusual expression, and for the deep exploration of unique experience may be misplaced. Television takes us into that which is already known, widely shared, meaningful in its familiarity. But that hardly diminishes the sense of variation that we can find there. In seeing how each new, individual instance of the formulas works itself out within the pattern of the familiar, we come to understand the pattern *and* the new form in more powerful ways. Television, then, can be seen as redressing an imbalance in our attitude toward the role of art in our lives, an imbalance in place perhaps since the Renaissance, certainly since the Romantic period. With television we are taught, or reminded, that our valorization of stunning individuality in art may be an aberration rather than the norm.

Magnum is interesting not only because of how he is like all other detectives but also in how, in that likeness, he shows me more of what is available in being a detective. Thus, I knew he was distinctively warm, human, vulnerable, open, and caring before I knew of any particular theological reasons for those qualities. Because the story continued, I could explore the reasons, the sources, the grounds for those qualities, without having to come to full closure.

　　We may conclude, then, by likening our value of novelty and innovation to a value of certain forms of religious speech and action, to the prophetic, and perhaps to the transcendent. We can liken our recognition of repetition and serial to notions of the priestly, the familiar, and perhaps the immanent. The deepest religious implication of television is that so long as its stories need not end, so long as it shows us the continuation and exploration of repetitive human experience, it shows us a theology of hope. In this way it becomes much like sacred scripture of all sorts. We wait for the Messiah to come, for the Messiah to come again, for the warrior's paradise, for true Enlightenment. We wait, knowing that we must live as if the event were to occur today and knowing that if it does not, we will live tomorrow as if that will be the day. The value of conventional fictions with strong endings and of television's small endings is that they allow us to imagine the consequences of actions. The value of serials is that they allow us to imagine that in spite of those consequences, there is still hope for change tomorrow.

# Television and Public Virtue

**ROBERT S. ALLEY**

An "event" occurred February 22, 1988, when CBS broadcast Linda Bloodworth-Thomason's "Designing Women" script "How Great Thou Art." The episode, a treatment of the role of women in Christian churches, was a brilliant example of current events folded into a comedic series form. It was startling in its realism, warm in its presentation, and absolutely hilarious in its dialogue. For those viewers reared in a Southern Baptist environment it had the added quality of nostalgia with its specific references to historical figures and organizational structures. Alice Ghostley, as Bernice Clifton, joined Jean Smart, as Charlene Frazier, to challenge the latter's minister in his opposition to the ordination of women. With the skill born of long years of Bible study, Bernice jousted with the preacher, trading Bible quotes verse for verse. Along the way Bernice found occasion to chide Roman Catholic priests, who, she suggested, by remaining unmarried, were in violation of the Scriptures. The show closed with Charlene informing her minister that she could no longer attend his church because he would deny young girls the dream of receiving ordination in an institution so influential in their childhood. "It's not my faith in God I'm worried about; it's my faith in you," she said to "Reverend Nunn." He argued, "We should not question God's wisdom." Charlene responded, "I'm not; I'm questioning yours!"

In television's history a traditional religious dimension

can be discovered in isolated incidents. From the earliest television series, family life was presumed to have a religious content. This is clear for the Protestant immigrants in "Mama," the Jewish homilies of Molly Goldberg in "The Goldbergs," and the Catholic family of "Life with Luiqi." Beaver went to Sunday School and Andy Griffith made much of his family's church affiliation. The Waltons went to church and often had a minister on the scene. Likewise, "Little House on the Prairie" included religious activity.

Different in character were frequent episodes of "Maude," "One Day at a Time," and "All in the Family" (when Norman Lear was at his best) that approached the forthright style of "Designing Women." And Father Mulcahy of "M\*A\*S\*H" did, once in a while, fight the religious system. These and isolated incidents on "The Smothers Brothers Comedy Hour" and "SOAP" provided a new foundation upon which to challenge an unnatural silence.

Then "Designing Women" broke the mold. The remarkable talent of Bloodworth-Thomason has set a new standard for addressing a sensitive subject. This unique accomplishment did not involve the selling of a specific dogma or doctrine but relied instead upon an open-minded, democratic humanism, fashioned with a sensitive feminist perspective. Jim Brooks commented in 1975 that "it's exciting when you can do a television show that flirts with the edges of art, and that happens every once in a while. . . . there are moments like that, especially in comedy, and that is when you can be proud."[1] His remarks concerning "The Mary Tyler Moore Show" apply unreservedly to the "Designing Women" episode.

It is in such rare moments that one may most easily identify a kind of democratic humanism at work in the best of television scripts. It is a humanism with roots in various religious and philosophical traditions woven into the fabric of our Republic. Such humanism begins with an appreciation of the values, real and potential, in human life. The Christian martyr Dietrich Bonhoeffer, shortly before his execution by the Nazis in 1945, wrote that "people are more important in life than anything else. . . . One can, of course, speak like that only if one has found others in one's life."

Martin Buber wrote of "I-Thou" relationships and Sir Thomas More was secure in believing that one "constructs a ladder" to deity "through knowledge of things natural." Ralph Waldo Emerson spoke of "the power" in all efforts at reform being anchored in "the conviction that there is an infinite worthiness in man which will appear at the call of worth."

Clearly, not all television producers and writers have shared such values, yet the peculiar fact is that when such sentiments do appear, they are more regularly the target of the religious dogmatist. This humanism seems to disturb that minority who foster doctrines of literal Original Sin and make exclusive claims to revelation and truth. Tolerance is not in their vocabulary, for they arrogate to themselves power from their particular version of God to explain absolutely what the Bible means. Enlightened humanism is, then, too close to home.

In 1985 the National Federation for Decency issued the claim that it was "a Christian organization promoting the Biblical ethic of decency in the American society with primary emphasis on television and other media." A careful examination of the *National Federation for Decency Journal* (hereinafter referred to as *NFDJ)* reveals that the opinions, ideas, and definitions contained therein are almost exclusively those of Donald E. Wildmon, a Methodist clergyman in Mississippi.

Wildmon, who frequently exposes his anti-Jewish bias, does employ the buzz phrase "Judeo-Christian heritage," but it is always clear that by using it Wildmon sought only to counter his critics while, in fact, asserting that Jewish ethics and values were only valid when filtered through belief in Jesus as God. Wildmon unquestionably believes television is not anti-Jewish, only anti-Christian. His own proclivities respecting Jewish citizens are made clear in an editorial in March 1985. He quoted a study done by Litcher and Rothman indicating that 59 percent of "the people who are responsible for network television programs were raised in Jewish homes."

The term "biblical ethics" is the linchpin of Wildmon's attack against television. The presumption is that there is one understood and accepted ethic from the Bible. Wildmon informs his readers that he comprehends the total meaning of Jesus' ethic and knows how to apply it. There is never a doubt in his mind as he goes on his search-and-destroy missions against network programming. He accepts the notion of an infallible Bible. This is the key to any absolutist view of ethics and theology. First, establish the source as God ordained. Second, claim the power from God to explain what the source means. Using that style Martin Luther admonished "loyal" citizens to "hew, stab and slay" the obstinate peasants because the Bible says, "It is better to cut off one member without mercy than to have the whole body perish by fire, or by disease" (Matthew 5:29–30). When Wildmon employs this tactic, he is espousing a view of the Bible rejected by millions of persons in America who call themselves Christians. For him to claim that there is a single clear inerrant biblical ethic on complex human problems related to government, religious diversity, sexuality, education, and popular art merely demonstrates his inability to comprehend the range of human potential in a free society.

Sadly, it is against this backdrop that popular attitudes about the television industry are frequently developed. A dose of the *National Enquirer* and Donald Wildmon can poison the culture most effectively. It must be asked, in a diverse and pluralistic democracy consisting of dozens of discrete publics, which self-styled group of "true believers" has the right to impose on others their own definitions? In the real world Wildmon merely expresses the views of one minority when he speaks of his biblical ethic. He cannot in good conscience claim, for he knows better, that the Christian population in this country is of one mind on the television programming he addresses.

Wildmon personifies a widespread effort in the political arena today to discredit humanism, a philosophy that, in point of fact, has a richly textured fabric and whose adherents include theists as well as nontheists. Indeed, it is the beauty of humanism that it provides a common meeting ground for Christian and non-Christian in a pluralistic society. The bitter attacks on humanism fail to comprehend that richness, as well as its history which demonstrates a natural affinity with many interpretations of the Christian faith.

As citizens, viewers, and makers of television alike, we seem constantly to be searching for an elusive "public virtue" or democratic way that can avoid dogmatism on the one hand and total relativism on the other. Daniel Boorstin locates "public virtue" in the "courage to doubt," a courage more precious than the courage of "the true believer . . . [who] makes himself the court of last resort on the most difficult matters on which wise men have disagreed for millennia." The Founders of our nation, Boorstin argues, had "a faith in the wisdom of mankind but a doubt of the wisdom of orthodox man. Their spirituality, their God, was a God of common human quest and not the God of anybody's dogma."

And this brings us back around to television. As "the most popular art" and the most powerful, it consumes us to a remarkable degree. The hegemony of the networks may be fading, but network programming remains and will remain for the foreseeable future the heart of the public's home entertainment fare. Does it convey values? Or was the cited episode of "Designing Women" an exception? There is no doubt in my mind that while Linda Bloodworth-Thomason is exceptional, her writing belongs to a long-standing tradition. I think Gene Roddenberry is on the mark when he reminds us that "all writers are concerned with values. That is what writing is all about." But not all persons in the creative community of television "care" about such matters.

Alan Alda identified this demarcation when he noted that "there are some persons in television who care enough about the society in which they live that they will not poison the system. It may be from such persons that we can expect to find good values in television." When pressed about the nature of those values, he stated it succinctly: "believing that people come first."

The following examples, drawn from fourteen years of interviews, delineate how some of those who care about society have defined "good values" in basically humanistic terms. The remarks cited do not apply uniformly to all works produced by these persons, for who among us possesses ideals that are consistently and regularly realized? Nevertheless, they provide a sense of direction that has energized television creativity at its best.

In a 1976 conversation with Alda, he was quite candid concerning his understanding of the medium of television. "I think that television has an enormous effect on us. . . . I think television is an educational medium. It is constantly transmitting a set of values to us, whether it knows it or not, or whether we know it or not. . . . It is probably more random than it is good or evil." Those values, for Alda, include the dangers inherent in violence, wherein we might be risking "a generation of sociopaths." Like most of his colleagues, he abhors censorship but "is very much in favor of responsible behavior." He means by this, "as a fellow-person, to suggest to other creative people to examine their view of reality."

My challenging friend Dick Levinson is motivated by the courage to doubt. With his brilliant partner, Bill Link, he created social dramas spanning the range of Bill of Rights issues, from "My Sweet Charlie" to "That Certain Summer" to "The Storyteller" to "The Guardian" to "Terrorist on Trial: The United States vs. Salim Ajami." Yet Dick was cautious about claiming to espouse "values." In 1976 he agreed that "you have to have some awareness that you may have influence," but he reminded me that the chief goal was to entertain. Nevertheless, he agreed that television has a liberal caste. "There aren't any shows putting down welfare. . . . I might say that there is a liberal caste because it is the right attitude that any enlightened person would have. One could make that statement." And Bill Link, reflecting on "My Sweet Charlie," confirms this perspective, noting that "the query What can be done about eliminating racial prejudice? is a different one from What can be done about those niggers?"

It was just these considerations about impact and values that haunted Dick during the months before completing his last dramatic work, "Terrorist on Trial: The United States vs. Salim Ajami." As we took a leisurely walk down Duke of Gloucester Street in colonial Williamsburg in the summer of 1986, he asked me what kind of reactions to Israel and its supporters might result from making the film. "We have perhaps five million Arabs living in this country. How are they going to feel about it?" He mused, "Suppose the audience misses our point, or suppose we make a point that generates undesirable consequences. Maybe we shouldn't make it." Two months later, in Hollywood, Dick and Bill were still raising questions. Bill asked, "Will this have social repercussions?" Dick continued, "The American public hates terrorists. Is it our job to tell them, have we a right to tell them, that there are two sides to terrorism? . . . If you want to deal with the subject honestly, then you have to make that defense." Out of their ingrained courage to doubt, Levinson and Link crafted an exceptional drama based upon a belief in the democratic process and freedom, a drama that saw ultimate "value" in due process.

A new generation of producers is reflected in P. K. Knelman, who shared production responsibilities on "Cagney and Lacey" from its beginning. She frankly stated: "I feel a personal need to take a stand in terms of my work. The work reflects my values, my political conscience. If we started doing stories just about the crook getting away and there was no underlying meaning, it would be quite a different thing. . . . I think that all our audience would not like it if we stopped having a political conscience." Knelman also commented on the feminine perspective: "I think that maybe women are uniquely equipped to connect with people because of their not being competitive. . . . Once in a while the show does hit on those things that make the women better qualified to do a job without the competitive male factor."

From an earlier era the late Quinn Martin, the consummate mogul, remarked, "Whether I was liberal, conservative, moderate, whatever, you can have an overall point of view, but you shouldn't use your vehicle to try to do a polemic." David Victor was more specific. "I think a producer, above all, is a human being in his own right. And all the things that he's lived through, all the things he's learned in his life must affect his particular philosophy and affect the way he operates." It was obvious that Victor's own background and his pride in his family were particularly significant in determining what he would do, *and* not do. John Mantley believes that the best shows he did "all said something about the human condition." Earl Hamner, the creator of "The Waltons," has no apology for asserting his interest in the representation of family solidarity and good values.

Norman Lear took it a step further when he affirmed that "as a full grown human being with children and concerns and attitudes, one who reads a couple of newspapers a day and pays attention to what is happening to the younger generation, of course the values and points of view I have affect my work. And why shouldn't they?" His last two series, "Palmerstown, U.S.A.," a story about a black child and a white child growing up as friends in the South during the depression, and "a.k.a. Pablo," a series devoted to the life of a Mexican-American family with its strong devotion to values of family unity, are testimony to this unapologetic commitment.

Garry Marshall, whose style and humor are so engaging one almost neglects to ask the "right" questions, said, "I think each creator's series has a certain vision, or a certain point of view. My shows are entertainment with an occasional social comment. . . . I pretty much stick to basic values of the family unit." As he effectively punctuates his points with wit and laughter, inserting comments about his children, you have little doubt about his genuineness and his dedication to a humanist perspective.

Marian Rees spoke recently of being "very proud to be a part of the television industry." She commented on her award-winning "Love Is Never Silent," noting that she "incorporates much of what was so compelling for me into the work I do." Looking back to her involvement with "The Autobiography of Miss Jane Pittman," Marian wondered whether "we hadn't in some way addressed, on an affective level, the personalization of the civil rights issues; not the proclamations but the persuasion to the heart and to the sensibility of who we are as people."

Alan Alda, citing the importance of style, talked about the power of television, observing: "I think the effect it has on us is at it greatest when the values that are transmitted to us are unspoken values." In particular, Alda was concerned about negative values: "Aggression is always at someone's expense, that you only succeed through someone else's loss." He resists heavy emphasis upon competition and lack of concern for cooperation. "I try to get writers and producers to present a more positive image of women on television, to try to examine the old ideas of the woman as victim as appropriate entertainment. It doesn't entertain me to see a woman harassed and terrorized. It does not entertain me to see a woman stand by and pour coffee and not be a part of the decision-making process. I don't think that is a true picture of women."

One of the earliest persons to sense the need to "say something" in a series may have been Loretta Young. "The reason I was doing this show ["The Loretta Young Show," 1953–1961] was to get a good idea into the mainstream of life. It was my whole point." As she looks back, she feels she was correct in her decision. "I hit more people. A lot of people didn't agree with me, with my answers to these problems, but that's their business. It was my program. They could go out and get another program and give you their point of view. . . . I won't propagandize something that I don't believe in. . . . It's my show, my name is up there, so it's got to stand for what I think."

One is reminded of the line in Link and Levinson's "The Storyteller." Writer Ira Davidson explains why he will no longer write stories about vehicular mayhem. Chided by the producer as caving in to pressure, Davidson responds: "I said what I am doing. What you do is your own business." Of course, for Link and Levinson censorship was not the answer; for them, good judgment and taste guided freedom. Young does not agree: "You must have censorship in the entertainment world or you will get pornography. You can't depend . . . on good taste."

Young is not alone in her concern about excesses. While few of those quoted here support censorship, many demonstrate concern that some type of internal oversight be exercised. Alda highlighted the dilemma: "I don't think censorship should be held as a threat against people who are seen not behaving responsibly. . . . And yet here I am saying I think we ought to express values that would help us as a group."

The humanism of the creative community has become, for large numbers, a public affirmation. Georgia Jeffries, writer for "Cagney and Lacey," spoke recently to a gathering of the Richmond Junior League on the subject of violence on television. She was candid in asserting: "What bothers me is that television reflects not only the realities of your lives, but also your dreams, your fantasies, and even on occasion your worst nightmares. . . . Films and television are the powerful literature of our day. Like all literature, it exists for two reasons: because the creators have a need to express ideas, and because, for people like me, there is a market that pays in exchange for those ideas. If you don't like the ideas expressed, don't buy the product." For her, television must not deny its part in the problems the society faces, but it must not be expected to accept all the blame. She believes it "is time for change in our values, before another generation goes by." She "wants to touch people in order to make a difference in the community." She commends series like the "Cosby Show," "Family Ties," "L.A. Law," and "St. Elsewhere" and observes that the makers of these series "care deeply about the work and its impact." Asked to define what constitutes good work she concludes that it involves "human feelings," "social conscience," and the exposure of "the evils of sexual harassment . . . and discrimination of all kinds."

Humanism, democracy, freedom, responsibility—all terms that seem compatible, but in the real world of television production it is not so easy. Gary Goldberg, creator of "Family Ties," commented: "I don't want to have somebody call in and say, 'You just violated everything I hold sacred.' You know, that would be very disturbing, so we constantly have the dilemma of trying to push ourselves as writers, trying to examine things that are really going on in society, and yet feel we have to have some caution about the people who are watching."

Jim Brooks was pondering these questions ten years earlier. "I don't believe anybody has a noble plan for television. I just think it is wide open for whatever works. There won't be violence when it's not working. And then I can think of why everything I just said is wrong, because I'm also recalling when CBS had an edict that you had to put black people in your shows. It was terrific pressure and that was something we needed. . . . I don't think anybody has answers, and if I keep talking now I'll start to say something that sounds like an answer, and I don't have one." Maude Findlay would probably respond, "God will get you for that!" In truth, Brooks had "answers" he has shared in "The Mary Tyler Moore Show," "Rhoda," "Taxi," and "The Associates." So do, and did, all those persons whose words seem to confirm Grant Tinker's hope that at its best television seeks to "open up the mind a little bit."

# 4   Network News Coverage of Religion

## JUDITH M. BUDDENBAUM

As they compete with each other for members, money, and influence, many religious organizations have learned to use the media to attract attention, gain members, and influence public policy.[1] If any religious group could translate its vision for society into public policy, that policy would affect everyone, not just group members. Therefore, people expect news coverage of religiously inspired activities and policy proposals. But the religion news people get from mass media, particularly from television, is problematic.

As a relatively new mass medium, television has become another focus for ideological disputes. On the one hand are optimists, who see television as a way to educate and enlighten the masses. They generally believe in a marketplace of ideas and assume that national television broadcasting will ultimately bring about understanding, consensus, and even "truth."[2] On the other hand are pessimists, who see television as dangerous because it "presents a fairly non-representative, non-concrete, imagined world" that is inherently at odds with the reality of life as most people live it.[3] In this pessimistic view, television news causes problems because it creates an image of the world on which people may act but which may not correspond to reality.

Although most Americans say television is their primary news source and believe it is more credible than newspapers,[4]

**57**

they also have trouble understanding television news. Robinson documents an increased sense of anomie since the advent of the nightly Huntley-Brinkley news report. That anomie is strongest among the least-educated, most television-reliant portions of the audience.[5] Although Robinson attributes this anomie partly to the way news is presented on television, the demographics of those who are disaffected but who rely heavily on television news are similar to the demographics of conservative church members who are technological pessimists.[6]

Therefore, it is not surprising that the conservative churches have frequently criticized television in general as well as its religion news content. Although optimistic spokespersons for churches sometimes complain about inaccurate stories or call for more news about church doctrine, they rarely find ideological bias or question the image of religion that is presented. Instead, they generally call for media scrutiny of all aspects of religion, even if it is unflattering to the church. As one Methodist editor said, "If we allow church bureaucracies to hold closed meetings or tell us what we can report, we're false prophets. We shouldn't be blind boosters for our cause."[7]

But "boosterism" is precisely what more conservative churches want. In his strident critique replete with numerous examples of religion news stories that were missed or bungled, Cal Thomas attributes the problem to "journalists . . . unable to identify with religious ideas, and . . . hostile or apathetic toward people who do."[8] Similarly, only 19 percent of Catholic priests surveyed said the press is "fair, honest or objective" in handling religion news. As one priest put it, the press is "interested only in the sensational, the shocking, the scandalous and not particularly in the more staid and less dramatic. This assessment is far more true in respect to television people."[9]

More moderate voices among the pessimists also equate "better coverage" with "more good news told about us and from our perspective." Billy Graham has called on reporters to "hold up a mirror to the young people of America." Covering positive role models, he says, is essential for the "moral fiber of America."

Although he asks for "more and better" news coverage of religion, his message suggests the media should reflect evangelical Christianity as the true faith, with other variants excluded or labeled as unacceptable.[10] Similarly, a *Christianity Today* report on a religion reporter for a Texas television station suggests that more stations should hire Baptists and allow them to report from a Baptist perspective.[11]

Reporters themselves have joined the debate over the quality of religion news coverage. Sometimes they tell their own horror stories in strong language, but they rarely detect bias in the news or suggest reporting from a particular religious perspective. As optimists, they recommend more investigative reporting, increased attention to diverse religious groups, or greater emphasis on doctrine and issues instead of personalities, events, and human-interest stories.[12]

A few journalists, however, echo the complaints of the pessimists. In a general critique of television, Michael Novak points out that "the myth of 'enlightenment' from local standards and prejudices still dominates our images of self-liberation and sophistication. . . . Television keeps pressing on the barriers of cultural resistance to obscenities, to some forms of sexual behavior, and to various social understandings. . . . The celebration of 'new moralities' may not lead to the kind of 'humanization' cultural optimists anticipate."[13]

Like Novak, Joseph Duggan, an editorial-page editor for the Richmond, Virginia, *Times-Dispatch,* attributes problems with news to the nature of the media and to standard journalistic methods, which create a secular mind-set in journalists. Duggan accuses journalists of practicing "vulgar Marxism" because they use "invidious class-based comparisons" in their reporting and exhibit "antipathy or indifference toward the spiritual side of man and to that which transcends earthly life and human nature." Their "fail[ure] to admit authentic religious content . . . into public discourse" in effect "concedes secular humanism . . . to be the common ground of the American experience."[14]

Because studies of religion news coverage have been

limited almost exclusively to the print media, it is difficult to evaluate criticisms of television coverage. Most content analyses of network news ignore religion as a category; others use the "religion" category only when no other possibility for coding a story exists. Although studies generally report that fewer than 2 percent of the stories concern religion, that probably underestimates the total volume of stories that actually mention religion.[15] In a study of television news coverage of international affairs, for example, Larson does not use religion as a category, but his work indicates that approximately 1 percent of the stories on each network between 1972 and 1981 covered the Vatican, while about one-third came from other trouble spots associated with religion, such as Northern Ireland, Iran, and the Middle East.[16]

Although Larson's work suggests there may be more network news stories mentioning religion than critics imagine, a few studies suggest problems in the way network news depicts religion. In a qualitative study of press coverage by two elite newspapers, two news magazines, and the three networks, Fields found that the media both "legitimated and delegitimated" the New Christian Right. She attributes this paradox to competing visions of what America is and should be: "The New Christian Right's programs violate political and religious norms [e.g., First Amendment concerns for freedom of religion, freedom of speech and press] while the techniques of the movement were consistent with pluralistic politics. . . . Therefore, the movement was depicted as effective on technical grounds, but not generally legitimate."[17]

Giving further credence to the pessimists' complaints, a study by *TV Guide* says religion news is "both neglected and distorted" partly because "fully 50 percent of television newspeople queried about their religion . . . answered 'none.' " That study found an overemphasis on the power and influence of Christian fundamentalists and on the color and excitement surrounding papal tours.[18]

In a study of crisis coverage that happens to include two religion-related crises—the Peoples' Temple massacre in Jonestown, Guyana, and the Iranian hostage crisis—Nimmo and Combs imply that the networks' approach to certain stories may cause some viewers to react negatively to the images of religion the networks create. The authors find that ABC uses "good grief journalism," CBS uses "fight journalism," and NBC uses "aw shucks journalism." ABC, they say, presents the image of an irrational world beyond the control of anyone. This suggests to the audience that the sane response is to say "good grief" and flee from the world. CBS emphasizes facts, figures, and reports from experts, thus underscoring the validity of Walter Cronkite's "that's the way it is" sign-off. This approach creates the image that viewers "know the facts" and have "a fighting chance" of finding solutions. NBC suggests that "aw shucks," nothing is new; everything is related to something else: "Each crisis has a long history and is embedded in a social, political, economic, religious and human context." However, NBC rarely explains connections, leaving viewers to interpret the relations for themselves.[19]

These studies suggest that religion news coverage is more extensive than many critics believe, but they also support the charge of bias that other critics make. In order to evaluate these arguments, I analyzed the religion news coverage of ABC, CBS, and NBC during three constructed months,[20] one each for 1976, 1981, and 1986. I asked five questions:

1. How much religion news is there?
2. Is the coverage evenly distributed among religions or are some covered much more extensively than others?
3. What information about religion do the stories provide?
4. How do the networks tell religion news stories? Do they use the presentation styles Nimmo and Combs found in crisis news for their general coverage of religion? Are there other stylistic elements that could interfere with understanding or that viewers could interpret as bias?
5. Has religion news increased over time and has it changed in information content or style?

I defined religion news as any story that mentions a religion, religious institution, or religious person or that uses religious language (e.g., "holy") or shows a religious person, institution, or symbol (e.g., a cross) in a way that suggests something about religion. After identifying religion stories in *TV News Index and Abstracts,* I examined the videotapes and eliminated stories that did not meet the definition of religion news to obtain my final sample of 240 stories.[21]

## Religion and News

Religion news is a surprisingly stable commodity. Not only were there few differences among the networks during any of the years included in the study, but there was little change over time.

Although the networks moved toward fewer but longer stories between 1976 and 1986 and the daily news hole decreased by at least one minute over the same period on all networks except ABC, the amount of religion news remained about the same. Religion was mentioned on between one-half and three-fourths of the newscasts by all networks in all years, and the total number of stories and the time devoted to them remained relatively constant (table 4.1).

Except in 1976, NBC provided a slightly higher proportion of stories (about 10 percent) and devoted slightly more of the news hole to them (12 to 15 percent) than did the other networks. NBC also devoted more time to religion in 1981 and 1986 than did ABC and CBS. However, the differences among the networks and over time are small and inconsistent. Stories with a holiday theme account for much of the change, because the networks carried newscasts on Christmas Day in 1981 and 1986 but not in 1976.

Although mentioning religion in between 6 and 11 percent of the stories and devoting between 7 and 15 percent of the news hole to them seems to provide a rather significant amount of religion news, the actual coverage was much less. Indeed, only CBS in 1976 and NBC in 1981 devoted more than 5 percent of the news

Table 4.1. Allocation of news hole to religion news by year and network

| Allocation | 1976 | | | 1981 | | | 1986 | | |
|---|---|---|---|---|---|---|---|---|---|
| | ABC | CBS | NBC | ABC | CBS | NBC | ABC | CBS | NBC |
| Total number of days in sample | 19 | 18 | 15 | 27 | 28 | 30 | 29 | 29 | 30 |
| Days with religion news, % | 52.6 | 72.2 | 73.3 | 55.6 | 57.1 | 76.7 | 48.3 | 75.0 | 73.3 |
| Total number of stories on days in sample | 293 | 279 | 208 | 398 | 415 | 399 | 313 | 375 | 371 |
| Stories mentioning religion, % | 6.1 | 8.2 | 7.2 | 6.3 | 6.5 | 10.5 | 7.3 | 7.7 | 10.0 |
| Average news hole per day in sample, in minutes and seconds | 22:10 | 22:50 | 22:30 | 22:20 | 23:00 | 21:40 | 22:00 | 21:40 | 21:20 |
| Total time devoted to religion news stories, % | 8.6 | 14.0 | 12.3 | 7.1 | 9.2 | 11.6 | 11.7 | 10.8 | 14.7 |
| Time actually devoted to mention or discussion of religion, % | 1.8 | 6.7 | 2.4 | 5.0 | 3.4 | 5.8 | 2.9 | 4.0 | 5.1 |

hole to actual coverage of religion (table 4.1). The mean *story* length was 2 minutes, 13 seconds; the median was 2 minutes. However, the mean time actually spent *on religion* was 51 seconds and the median length was only 30 seconds.

Besides providing very little time for actual news about religion, the networks paid little attention to most religions. In all years, Catholicism was mentioned in at least one-fifth of the stories on all networks. While non-Christian religions were sometimes mentioned in a similar proportion of stories, occasional heavy attention to Protestants is misleading because stories about them are divided among several denominations. Most individual Protestant denominations are almost invisible to network viewers (table 4.2).

This pattern of attention to various religious traditions depends on the geographic origin of the news stories. In fact, the tradition receiving heaviest emphasis in each year is the direct result of the foreign news during that year. Except for NBC in 1976 and ABC in 1986, about half of the news concerned religion in foreign countries. Although the countries emphasized changed over time, most are traditional religious trouble spots (table 4.3). In 1976 about one-fourth of the stories were from Lebanon; most were told in terms of fighting between Moslems and unspecified Christians. As a result, more stories mentioned those groups in 1976 than in any other year. In 1976 and again in 1981 significant attention went to fighting in Northern Ireland between Catholics and Protestants, but the 1981 sample also included many stories about the Catholic church's involvement in Polish politics. Thus, Catholic coverage was particularly high in 1981. In 1986 the Middle East was back in the news because Americans Father Lawrence Jenco and the Reverend Benjamin Weir were held hostage in Lebanon and then released. The Philippines and South Africa also moved to center stage; therefore, Catholic coverage remained high. However, news of mainline Protestants increased significantly because of references to Anglican envoy Terry Waite and to the Reverend Benjamin Weir, a Presbyterian, in news of the hostage crisis and because of heavy reliance on the Anglican archbishop The Most Reverend Desmond Tutu as an antiapartheid source in news from South Africa.

**Table 4.2. Religions mentioned in religion news stories by year and network (in percentages)**

| Religion | 1976 | | | 1981 | | | 1986 | | |
|---|---|---|---|---|---|---|---|---|---|
| | ABC (n = 18) | CBS (n = 23) | NBC (n = 15) | ABC (n = 25) | CBS (n = 27) | NBC (n = 42) | ABC (n = 23) | CBS (n = 29) | NBC (n = 38) |
| **Christian** | | | | | | | | | |
| Christian (unspecified type) | 44.5 | 21.7 | 40.0 | 8.0 | 18.5 | 16.7 | 17.4 | 10.3 | 10.5 |
| Protestant (unspecified type) | 11.1 | 4.3 | — | 4.0 | 3.7 | 9.5 | 8.7 | 17.4 | 18.4 |
| Mainline Protestant | — | 4.3 | — | 8.0 | 7.4 | 4.8 | 30.4 | 17.4 | 21.1 |
| Evangelical Protestant | 16.7 | 17.4 | 6.7 | 16.0 | 11.1 | 9.5 | 8.7 | 6.9 | 10.5 |
| Holiness Protestant | — | — | — | — | — | 2.4 | — | — | — |
| Latter Day Saints | 5.6 | 4.3 | 6.7 | — | — | — | — | — | — |
| Roman Catholic | 22.3 | 21.7 | 20.0 | 40.0 | 44.4 | 47.7 | 30.4 | 41.3 | 39.5 |
| Orthodox Catholic | — | — | — | — | 3.7 | 2.4 | — | — | — |
| **Non-Christian** | | | | | | | | | |
| Jewish | 5.6 | 26.1 | 20.0 | 12.0 | 14.8 | 4.8 | 8.7 | 10.3 | 15.8 |
| Moslem | 11.1 | 17.4 | 33.4 | 12.0 | 3.7 | 7.2 | — | 3.4 | 5.2 |
| Hindu | — | — | — | 4.0 | — | — | — | 10.3 | 2.6 |
| Native American | — | — | — | 4.0 | — | — | — | — | — |
| Cults | — | — | — | 12.0 | 11.1 | 4.8 | 13.0 | 13.8 | — |

Note: Totals do not equal 100% because more than one religion could be mentioned in and coded for each story.

**Table 4.3.  Geographic location of sources of religion news by year and network (in percentages)**

| Location | 1976 | | | 1981 | | | 1986 | | |
|---|---|---|---|---|---|---|---|---|---|
| | ABC (n = 18) | CBS (n = 23) | NBC (n = 15) | ABC (n = 25) | CBS (n = 27) | NBC (n = 42) | ABC (n = 23) | CBS (n = 29) | NBC (n = 38) |
| United States | 50.0 | 47.8 | 60.0 | 48.0 | 37.0 | 47.6 | 52.2 | 27.6 | 36.8 |
| Foreign country | | | | | | | | | |
| Europe | | | | | | | | | |
| Northern Ireland | 11.1 | 4.3 | 6.7 | 4.0 | 3.7 | 7.2 | — | 3.4 | 2.6 |
| USSR | 5.6 | 4.3 | — | 4.0 | — | 2.4 | 4.3 | 3.4 | — |
| Vatican City | — | 4.3 | 6.7 | 16.0 | 11.1 | 16.7 | 8.7 | — | — |
| Other[a] | — | 4.3 | — | 8.0 | 14.8 | 7.2 | 4.3 | 13.8 | 15.7 |
| Middle East | | | | | | | | | |
| Lebanon | 33.3 | 26.1 | 26.7 | 4.0 | 7.4 | 7.2 | — | — | 2.6 |
| Other[a] | — | 4.3 | — | 12.0 | 11.1 | — | 4.3 | — | — |
| Africa[a] | — | — | — | — | — | — | 13.0 | 13.8 | 18.4 |
| Asia and Pacific islands[a] | — | 4.3 | — | 4.0 | 7.4 | 2.4 | 8.7 | 13.8 | 7.9 |
| Australia | — | — | — | — | — | — | — | 3.4 | 2.6 |
| Latin America and South America[a] | — | — | — | — | 3.7 | 7.2 | — | 10.3 | 5.3 |
| None[b] | — | — | — | — | 3.7 | 2.4 | 4.3 | 10.3 | 5.3 |

Notes: Differences among networks, 1976, 1981, 1986: $p$ = not significant. Differences within networks, ABC, CBS, NBC: $p \le$ .05. Totals do not equal 100% because of rounding.
[a]Countries not reported by at least two networks in each of two years.
[b]Stories in this category are general commentaries about religion.

This heavy emphasis on religion news from traditional foreign trouble spots also explains the information about religion that the networks provided. Most stories explored the relationship between religion and politics. Only scattered stories on the networks in 1976 and on NBC in 1981 paid much attention to religion in connection with subjects other than military activities and terrorism, government and international relations, or law, crime, and the courts. Substantive news about religion was rare. Information about religious doctrine and practices, church history, and the sociology of religion (demographics, trends, etc.) was given in fewer than one-fourth of all religion stories. Most of the rest emphasized people, political conflict, or specific events.

During 1976 the three networks broadcast fifty-six religion news stories, but the stories provided very little substantive information about religion. About four-fifths were really political stories. In many of those, the networks used religious labels interchangeably with political ones or used religious sources without enough explanation to make the information meaningful. This problem occurred most frequently in the foreign news. In those stories, the presentation also suggested the networks were taking sides in disputes among religious factions.

In seventeen stories from Lebanon, the networks used the labels "Christian" and "Moslem" along with political terms such as "right wing," "leftist," "Phalangist," "Palestinian," and "Arab" in a way that made it hard to tell who was fighting whom. Most stories also failed to explain the reasons for the war or why sides were drawn along quasi-religious lines. A few, however, gave brief but confusing explanations. On January 27, 1976, for example, CBS reporter Mike Lee said that Christians "see themselves as protecting their own religion" and "right wing Christians are fearful that a Palestinian presence here will threaten the sovereignty of the Lebanese government." But in a September 28 CBS story, Richard Threlkeld said, "Christian businessmen have visions of making Juniyah a kind of Mideast Monte Carlo and of leaving downtown Beirut and its Moslem conquerors to wither on the vine."

Although that comment about "Moslem conquerors"

might suggest bias to some viewers, CBS and NBC provided relatively balanced coverage. NBC stressed political positions and negotiations, making the situation seem manageable. Stories on January 27 and February 2 mentioned similar Christian and Moslem misgivings about the latest events and a similar goal: a democratic and essentially secular state with religious freedom for all. CBS provided more commentary and explanation than NBC, but it also more often showed the news from a Moslem perspective, as in an October 21 story. While the video cut from scenes of a devastated Moslem community to ones of Christian troops, correspondent Mike Lee reported, "The jovial mood among Christian gunmen is as if nothing was to be taken seriously." Lee paused, then concluded, "Nothing but dozens of shrapnel victims from last night."

However, in coverage of events in Lebanon, ABC made it clear that Moslems are the "bad guys" and Christians are "good guys"—or at least relatively innocent victims in a situation beyond anyone's control. The January 16 story, for example, began with Harry Reasoner reporting that Lebanese air force planes had strafed Moslems and Palestinians who were attacking the Christian town of Damour, but the story quickly cut to Jim Bennett in Lebanon. Against a backdrop of a Christian church, and with church bells ringing, Bennett explained, "Services were held for the dead, whom Palestinians say were victims of a massacre," before concluding, "There are only losses, never winners in a war of attrition." A similar use of "good grief" style showed up in a May 8 report that the Lebanese parliament had selected "Christian-backed banker" Elias Sarkis as the country's new president. The story ended with reporter Jim Bennett saying, "Sarkis won't solve and may start new problems."

The same problems of unexplained labels and bias showed up in network news of unrest in Northern Ireland. Again, ABC's "good grief" style suggested events out of control. On October 11, in a story about a peace movement led by Catholics Mairaad Corrigan and Betty Williams, Harry Reasoner said, rather condescendingly, "It's quite remarkable that two ordinary Catholic women have been able to unite the Catholics and Protestants in

Northern Ireland in the first nonsectarian mass protest in that divided province." Later, in response to a question from coanchor Barbara Walters about whether "any of this will make a difference," Reasoner replied, "I don't know whether it will in Ireland or not. The problem is you're dealing with the world's most attractive people that behave like idiots. . . . The men of passion do not respond to any rationality or compassion."

Most domestic religion news concerned the 1976 election. Although the networks rarely seemed to take sides, most of the thirteen stories contained the kind of unexplained labels or fragmentary explanations that permeated the foreign news.

Coverage focused on Jimmy Carter and his born-again religion. On October 11 the three networks carried similar stories about Carter's interview with *Playboy* magazine. In the ABC version, the video cut from campaign scenes to a shot of the Reverend W. A. Criswell, dressed in a business suit and standing at the pulpit in a large church. Reporter Tom Jarriel introduced Criswell as "pastor of the nation's largest Baptist church" and said that Criswell supported Ford because of the *Playboy* interview. Then, as vague church music died away, Criswell was shown telling his congregation, "There are other public media through which we can discuss the moral issues of life and government other than the pages of a salacious, pornographic magazine." Ten days later, all three networks aired Carter's reply: "Mr. Ford knows *Playboy* has interviewed many people . . . his own secretary of the treasury, Mr. Simon. . . . And I think it's highly misleading to insinuate that I'm a special case or that I have low morals because I granted an interview to *Playboy* magazine."

While the *Playboy* interview was in the news, NBC said that "Carter has another problem . . . with Illinois's big Catholic population" because of his stance on abortion. However, in one of the few substantive stories during the year, CBS gave viewers a quite different impression. Devoting nearly four minutes to the story, the network used charts and graphs to explain patterns in Catholic voting behavior. Reporter Chris Kelley acknowledged that Catholics are uneasy about Carter's "evangelical style," but in in-

terview segments, the Reverend Thomas Gannon, a Catholic sociologist, said, "Abortion is not an issue for Catholics in spite of
the church's [position] on the issue," and sociologist-novelist the
Reverend Andrew Greeley noted that Polish Catholics are unlikely
to support Ford because of his "goof concerning Poland."

During 1981 more stories provided substantive information about religion and depicted complex relationships between
religion and society than in 1976. In fact, only about one-fifth of
the stories resembled those in the 1976 sample, and almost all of
those were from the same religious trouble spots.

The dominant pattern during 1981 was one of detailed,
complex stories, suggesting that the networks had discovered religion to be an extremely useful device for furthering a story line or
adding color to the news. This new approach was most apparent in
the networks' heavy attention to international Catholicism. In fact,
the religion news during 1981 could appropriately be subtitled "The
Pope and Poland." Whereas Pope Paul VI showed up briefly in
only one story during 1976, Pope John Paul II appeared or was
mentioned in one-fifth of all stories during 1981.

Part of that coverage, of course, came as an unavoid-
able consequence of the attempt on the pope's life by Mehmet Ali
Agca. However, even there the coverage was so heavy, detailed,
and complex that it was almost obsessive. Eight stories on sample
dates between May 19 and July 22 practically canonized the pope
while portraying Moslems as irrational fanatics. On May 19, for
example, CBS and NBC showed close-ups of the pope's bandaged
hands and intravenous feeding tubes while reporting that he is
"much better." CBS mentioned Agca's "possible connections with
international terrorist organizations." NBC noted Agca had
planned to kill Queen Elizabeth II but backed off "because of his
ideology—however, police say he made that up." ABC illustrated
the segment about the pope's health with artist Gerald Andrea's
drawing of a drinking cup as Bill Blakemore reported the pope
"took his first food by mouth and his first walk." After mentioning
that Prime Minister Pierre Trudeau of Canada and a personal envoy from the Ayatollah Khomeini were in Rome to pay their re-

spects, Blakemore reported, "Franciszek Cardinal Marcharski of Kracow saw and prayed with the pope under a picture of the Madonna of Kracow—Poland's 'sacred madonna,' who is also the emblem of the Solidarity movement," as Andrea's drawing of the pope, the cardinal, and a picture of the madonna appeared on screen. After Blakemore noted that the cardinal "will probably be appointed the new archbishop of Poland," anchor Peter Jennings in New York said Agca also intended to kill Queen Elizabeth II. He did not, however, because he "discovered she's a woman" and "he's a Turkish Moslem and Moslems don't kill women."

The stories from June and July simply gave updates on the pope's health or on his fanatical would-be assassin. However, the assassination attempt accounted for only a fraction of the attention the pope received during 1981. Earlier in the year, the networks told detailed, complex stories about his Asian tour and used him as the centerpiece for religious stories on Good Friday.

In coverage typical for the year, all three networks showed the pope carrying a cross through the streets of Rome on Good Friday as he "symbolically retraced Christian steps . . . through ruins of the pagan Roman Empire . . . to remember those who suffer for their faith." ABC spliced in video from Jerusalem, which "is unusually crowded because Passover begins tomorrow." CBS anchor Dan Rather said, "Today, too, many suffer for their faith." Finally, as the sound of the pope, probably speaking Italian, rose and then fell, Rather concluded, "Because of Good Friday, the stock market is closed." In the NBC version, reporter Keith Miller added that the clergy "wear white and purple robes of mourning" and the "pope doesn't wear his papal ring, as another sign of mourning."

If the networks discovered the pope during 1981, they also found and were fascinated by Catholicism in Poland. Stories from there created an image of Soviet repression of religion, but they also clearly showed the power and influence of the church. In a Good Friday story about a new "rural Solidarity union," NBC devoted nearly thirty seconds of video to scenes of workers coming out of a meeting hall. The leader carried a large crucifix on a staff;

others carried rosaries, kissed the crucifix, and crossed themselves. Similarly, September 5 reports by CBS and NBC of Soviet military maneuvers on Poland's borders devoted long segments to scenes of Archbishop Jozef Glemp officiating at mass and of Solidarity leader Lech Walesa worshipping. CBS also let viewers listen to people singing "an old religious anthem" as reporter Doug Sefton developed the "Soviet religious repression" theme: "[The anthem] has a line that says 'God bless this free country,' but in the German occupation of World War II, it was changed to 'God bring us back our free country,' which is the way it was sung today."

The pope did not figure in most news from Poland, but he eventually became part of the story. On December 13 and on Christmas Day, the networks linked news of events in Poland with video of the pope's comments during worship services in Vatican Square and human interest features from Catholic churches in the United States.

Although native American beliefs, the Unification church, and the Rajneesh cult occasionally received thorough coverage, Protestants would have been nearly invisible during 1981 if the networks had not tried to balance their Christmas newscast by inserting clips of choirs singing in mainline churches. Only once did Protestants receive attention similar to that given Catholics.

On April 17 each network devoted approximately two minutes to tributes to boxer Joe Louis following his death. All seemed fascinated with the setting—an exhibition hall behind Caesar's Palace in Las Vegas—and with the famous people attending the funeral; all mixed video of the speakers, the choir, the audience, and the flower-covered casket on display in a boxing ring with historical footage from Louis's career.

ABC developed the most secular story line by cutting from Sammy Davis, Jr., singing, "Here's to Winners," to Frank Sinatra saying, "The man who never rested on canvas now sleeps on clouds," to the Reverend Jesse Jackson shouting, "Let's hear it for the champ," before ending with reporter Dick Schaap's "good grief" conclusion, "If it wasn't dignified, it worked." Although none of the networks identified Louis's religion or that of the speakers, CBS and NBC put Jackson's remarks in a religious context before showing him and the congregation in a traditional call and response:

> JACKSON: Death is not a time to mourn, but to celebrate the final victory. Let's hear it for the champ.
> CONGREGATION: shouts, murmurs. . . .
> JACKSON: Be glad about it. . . .
> CONGREGATION: Yes, amen, hallelujah. . . .

The rather thorough network religion coverage in 1981 did not continue into 1986. The presentation style in more than half the news reverted to the pattern of simple, unexplained mentions used during 1976. Although a few stories provided substantial attention to religion similar to that in 1981, the dominant pattern was one of using angles and evidence to discredit both beliefs and believers.

This new problem was most apparent on February 23, when ABC covered the opening of the Twenty-seventh National Party Congress in the Soviet Union with a feature portraying Lenin as a cult figure and the Soviet people as his blindly obedient disciples. Noting ringing bells in the background, reporter Walter Rodgers said, "The Kremlin bells call the faithful to the tomb of Lenin on a solemn pilgrimage much like medieval church bells called Christians to worship Christ in the holy shrines of Jerusalem." Then, as the video showed Lenin's tomb, busts of Lenin, and finally soldiers on parade in Red Square, he continued:

> Here Lenin lives in the present tense. . . . His revolution swept away the Russian Orthodox church and in the remaining vacuum, Lenin, who loathed idolatry, became the new Soviet messiah. And seventy years after the Bolshevik Revolution, Lenin's soldiers are still "marching as to war" with his scarlet "banners going on before. . . ." As the leader of the revolution, Lenin is portrayed as omniscient, unerring. . . . As there is room for only one political party, there is room for only one demigod in the Soviet pantheon of heroes.

Although that discrediting of the Soviet Union is understandable when set against the long history of strained U.S.-Soviet relations, about one-third of the stories used similar juxtapositions of information and images to create an impression of dangerous Christian meddling in politics and of Christians as hypocrites.

Only reports on all three networks during January and February of the events that brought Corazon Aquino to power in the Philippines displayed any of the fascination with the Catholic church and the attention to detail that permeated the 1981 news. But even those stories gave little information about the church. Instead, they used Catholic clergy primarily to comment on the political situation. While CBS and NBC provided the most extensive coverage and made the most use of religious sources, the juxtaposition of scenes of both average people and the Marcos family worshipping suggested both sides were merely using religion for political purpose.

A stronger image of the Catholic church meddling in the internal politics of a nation occurred during reports of civil unrest in Haiti. A February 2 story on NBC reported that the Haitian government blamed the Catholic church and Protestant missionary groups for antigovernment violence in Port-au-Prince. In a February 23 CBS report, anchor Susan Spencer said, "Haiti's chief voodoo priest, Max Duvar, says the interim government favors the Catholic church. . . . He claims the government is risking a religious war." Neither story used a Catholic source to put the events in context.

In the United States, stories on CBS and NBC on May 8 showed the Catholic church challenging the U.S. government, while those on ABC and NBC in August presented the pope as an unwelcome and misguided meddler in American education. The CBS version of the May 8 story reporting that a New York court had found the U.S. Catholic Conference in contempt for failing to turn over documents to the court illustrated the story with a drawing of a bishop's miter with a scepter laid across it in a way that suggested the message "no bishops." On August 20 the networks reported the Vatican had stripped Father Charles Curran of his authority as a Catholic theologian because he failed to teach the church position on social issues as the only correct position. In the longer of the two versions, NBC followed Archbishop James Hickey's comment that the "church isn't based on democracy" with spokespersons from the Catholic University of America and Notre Dame University who expressed fears about the effect of the Vatican ruling on the church and church education in America.

Catholics were not the only ones portrayed negatively. On March 14, in a long and generally sympathetic report on the trial of Arizona Presbyterians and Lutherans involved in the sanctuary movement, CBS suggested sinister activity by showing people hiding their identity by wearing ski masks. In a July 31 feature on "The Selling of Ortega," ABC created a similar image of dangerous mainline meddling. Reporter Jeff Greenfield pointedly said that Daniel Ortega, the Sandinista president of Nicaragua, "also used his time [on a visit to the United States] to rally the faithful. At Riverside Church his host was one-time antiwar activist William Sloane Coffin and his audience also included a senior citizen of the American left, attorney William Kunstler." And on May 19, in one of the few stories about purely religious conflict, ABC made the Methodist church's concern for peace seem slightly ridiculous. In coverage of a proposal to eliminate militant songs from the church hymnal, reporter Jim Wooten developed the theme that "people attend church for the music" without supporting that assertion. Between clips of people singing "Onward Christian soldiers" and "Glory, glory, hallelujah, his truth is marching on," church spokesman Carlton Young explained, "We don't use those words if we are committed to being the Church of Jesus Christ, the Prince of Peace." However, the story ended with rebuttals from average church members, including a young boy who said he likes the songs and the church should "concentrate on the real causes of war," and Wooten's "good grief" assessment, "In this twentieth-century world of war and hunger and nuclear accidents and terrorism, to sing or not to sing is clearly not the question. But in a world of so few answers, it was bound to be asked."

Similar stories about evangelical Christians created the

impression that they, too, are slightly ridiculous and hypocritical, but also potentially dangerous meddlers. On April 9, for example, ABC covered the California senate race with a story that included video of actor Charleton Heston in the movie *The Ten Commandments* and juxtaposed clips of Eldridge Cleaver in 1968 calling for "armed revolution" and clips of him during his 1986 political campaign claiming to be a "born-again Reagan conservative."

CBS and NBC created a similar impression on October 21 in short stories devoted to "TV evangelist-cum-politician" Pat Robertson's libel suit against Congressman Andrew Jacobs and former Congressman Paul "Pete" McCloskey over their allegation that Robertson's father had helped him avoid combat duty during the Korean War. However, NBC led into the Robertson story with one about John DeLorean's trial for fraud and embezzlement. Because that story included the information that DeLorean "claims to have become a born-again Christian with a new purpose in life" and that he "wrote a book about his troubles and plugged it" on talk shows, the two-story package heightened the impression of hypocrisy.

## Conclusion

Network newscasts devote more attention to religion than critics imagine. Between 6 and 11 percent of all stories on each of the networks during the three years covered in this study mentioned religion. Religion news stories showed up in at least half of the newscasts.

Although that is probably as many religion news stories as one can reasonably expect, true religion news is rare. Fewer than one-fifth of the religion stories focused on religion. The rest mentioned religion as a minor element in an essentially secular context. The time actually spent on mentions or discussions of religion accounted for only 2 to 7 percent of the news.

Furthermore, the networks covered some religions much more extensively than others. Stories about Catholicism accounted for at least one-fifth of each network's coverage. Many of these stories were necessary because of the networks' emphasis on foreign news. However, others took advantage of the dramaturgical elements of Catholic worship and of Pope John Paul II as an easily identifiable, charismatic figure.

Too little attention is paid to other varieties of Christianity in U.S. news. Less than one-fifth of the stories on any network in any given year mentioned people and organizations associated with the evangelical tradition. About half of that went to the religious right. The rest focused on black Baptists. Pentecostals appeared in only one story from the Soviet Union; individual mainline Protestant denominations would have been equally invisible had it not been for mentions of Presbyterians and Anglicans in foreign news.

Similarly, the networks covered relatively few subjects. The networks provided more information about conflict and discrete events than about religion itself. And even their conflict- and event-oriented coverage was limited. Fully three-fourths of the stories concerned military conflict between religious factions or conflict between religion and secular political authority. Few stories explored primarily religious disputes within or among churches. Fewer than one-fourth provided significant information about religious beliefs and behavior.

Stories about Catholics and black Baptists generally provided the most information about beliefs and religiously inspired opinions on issues and the most images of people engaged in primarily religious activities, but none fully explained the theology that would account for these opinions and behaviors. In fact, most stories mentioning Protestants failed even to identify denominations to help viewers understand the story.

Although the three networks provided similar amounts of factual religion information, each network has a distinctive style. ABC's religion news portrayed religion as one more irrational force out of control. NBC explored the relationship between religion and more aspects of secular society, avoiding the simplistic explanations and commentary that showed up regularly on ABC.

CBS usually presented facts in a way that made the situations seem understandable. Explanations and comments were more common than on NBC, but they were more neutral than on ABC.

The networks fall short of their potential for providing a marketplace of ideas. Each provided some thorough, understandable, and meaningful stories each year. However, the networks do not take religion news seriously nor have they improved coverage over time. And although no religious traditions were singled out for hostile coverage, juxtaposed images and information too often cast aspersions on both beliefs and believers. Some stories in all years gave a feel for the power and importance religious people find in faith, but at least an equal number delegitimized religion and religiously inspired concerns and behavior.

# 5 Religious Television Spots

**JOHN P. FERRÉ**

𝕿he video begins with a young couple interested in buying the house that a realtor is showing to them.

> "Are there any blacks in the neighborhood?" asks the husband.
> "Absolutely not!"
> "You mean this is a restricted neighborhood?"
> "Absolutely!"
> "We've changed our minds," the wife replies. The couple leaves.[1]

> "Bless those who were unable to worship with us today," says the voiceover as the screen shows a congregation. "Because of problems"—the scene changes to a cartoon of a golfer. "Because of illness"—the scene changes to a cartoon of a sunbather. "And other hardships"—the final scene is a cartoon of men fishing.[2]

Although religious broadcasters considered using such video vignettes as early as 1950, there was no pressing need to produce them then. The networks donated blocks of time to the three central religious traditions in the United States: Protestants, represented by the Federal Council of Churches of Christ; Catholics, represented by the National Council of Catholic Men; and

Jews, represented by the Jewish Seminary of America. These mainline religious groups enjoyed free (sustaining) time and the use of network production facilities. Large evangelical denominations, turned away by the networks, were able to secure sustaining time from local stations. These noncontroversial religious programs helped broadcasters meet their public interest mandate and satisfy the religious groups' desire for public expression. By the end of the 1950s, nearly half of all religious television programming was broadcast during time that networks or local stations donated.[3]

The 1960s marked the beginning of a swift decline in free television time for religious groups. The decline began in 1960, when the Federal Communications Commission decided that sustaining time for religious programming did not serve the public interest any more than paid time did. The commission's decision removed what incentive the stations had to donate blocks of time to religious organizations. More and more time was for sale, the cheapest being the ghetto hours of Sunday morning. Free time for full-length programming all but vanished. Sustaining time began to consist primarily of spots for which advertisements had not been sold and for which the broadcaster had decided not to fill with a station or program promotion.[4]

As available time slots were shrinking from program to commercial length, the churches' attitude toward advertising was liberalizing, partly in response to the social environment of ecumenicism signified by Vatican II. Previously hesitant to advertise for fear of appearing divisive and sectarian, churches began to realize how much different traditions had in common. According to Lester F. Heins, former executive director of public relations for the American Lutheran Church, "The areas of agreement are so surprisingly broad that churches which formerly feared getting into public debate now find they can speak positively out of their own traditions without striking up bitter controversy."[5]

By 1977 only 8 percent of religious programs were broadcast on a sustaining basis.[6] Religious broadcasters were left with four options. They could operate their own stations at enormous cost; they could buy increasingly expensive blocks of time;

they could hope that stations would broadcast the public service announcements (PSAs) that they sent; or they could purchase advertising time. By and large, the costliest options, operating a station or buying blocks of time, were chosen by a small number of independent, evangelical personalities who received funds by appealing frequently for donations. Large mainline and evangelical organizations contented themselves with the wisps of time that stations donated or sold. Sustaining religious programs of length had become an anachronism.

## Advocates

Changes in broadcast policies and the rise of ecumenicism only partially explain the rise of religious television spots. Media enthusiasts advocated the production of religious vignettes for television almost from the beginning of the medium's commercial development. Advocates argued that paid advertisements and PSAs had certain advantages over full-length programming and that these spots could be used for various worthwhile purposes. In 1950 Edward J. Carnell of Fuller Theological Seminary wrote:

> One of the most promising outlets that even a local church can sustain is to devise a telecommercial, a sixty-second drama from life which vividly advertises both the gospel and the church which preaches it. These dramas, carefully filmed, can be presented over and over just as are the advertisements for cigarettes. Through this means the gospel can repetitiously reach ears and eyes in the parlors of the nation. Furthermore, such "shorts" can be produced with a minimum of expense.[7]

Carnell and others pointed out the advantages that PSAs have over full-length religious programs. Producing television programs for Sunday mornings requires that vast funds be spent for a time when relatively few people tune in. PSAs, on the other hand, air for free whenever stations have not sold advertising and are willing to forgo a station promotion. The spots are cheaper and reach more viewers. As J. Harold Ellens observes, "Some denominations decided that thirty seconds of prime time was better than an hour of ghetto time."[8]

The only costs of religious PSAs are those of production and distribution. Bonneville Media Communications in Salt Lake City, producer of high-quality Mormon spots, has almost cornered the market on airing religious PSAs across the country, because they are willing to spend $125,000 to $150,000 for the slickest productions. Producers of religious PSAs do pay high costs for production, but they avoid the even higher costs of airtime.

Spots have more advantages that just being cost-effective. Their brevity does not give viewers time to turn them off. Viewers can be ambushed; people who do not ordinarily watch religious programs see them. Moreover, television spots do not preempt regularly scheduled shows, so they do not invite audience hostility, as Billy Graham does each time he televises his crusades.[9]

Religious PSAs for television date back to 1958, when the Episcopal church produced its "Holy Day and Holiday" series. Through one-minute color presentations featuring great works of art, the Episcopalians explained the religious significance of Easter, Independence Day, Labor Day, Thanksgiving, and Christmas. First circulated in churches, this series was broadcast by NBC on prime time.[10]

Such early success motivated the Episcopal church to continue producing television spots. In the early 1960s, it produced "Thought for the Day" spots, in which a minister talked directly into the camera, but these were discontinued because they were unpopular. But persistence paid off. Another Episcopalian PSA, "Spectator Sport," was so popular that it ran even during a nationally televised ball game:

> "There's a lot of trouble in the world."
> [riots and burning city]
> "There really is!"

[contemplative viewer]
"And you can't make it go away by switching channels."
[blurred television screen]
"Being a Christian . . .
[lions and Christians in Roman amphitheater]
. . . didn't used to be a spectator sport."
[Roman Christians]
"It still isn't!"
[television viewer followed by name of sponsor]

Concise, dramatic, and clever, this video fully exploited the medium of television.[11]

The early masters of the medium for religious purposes were the Franciscans. Under the direction of Father Emery Tang, who conceived of television spots as nonsectarian mini–morality plays, such Franciscan PSAs as the one on neighborhood integration were broadcast by more than 750 stations in the United States, almost 300 in Canada, and some 50 in Australia.[12]

Evangelism is only one reason for producing PSAs; another is public relations. An early advocate of religious broadcasting wrote that television could be used to "break down prejudice and clear up misunderstanding toward the church and Christianity where these have existed."[13] Bonneville's Mormon spots are largely external public relations productions. According to Bonneville producer Ron Anderson, Mormon PSAs are designed to counter the belief, common outside Utah, that Mormons are stern, humorless, or reactionary.[14]

The Church of the Nazarene produced a series of PSAs for internal public relations. Besides countering a public impression that the denomination is cultic, their series meant to instill pride among Nazarenes. According to the Nazarenes' national spokesperson Russell Bredholt, "We want church members to see the ads and be able to say, 'Yes, that's us, and we like what we see.' "[15]

Besides evangelism and public relations, religious producers also make PSAs for moral reasons. Given the strong family values of the Mormons, it is no surprise that they champion the family in their advertisements. Their "Homefront" campaign dramatized misunderstandings between parents and teenagers. These spots proposed solutions to family communication problems and offered a free booklet of tips for enhancing communication between parents and children. The Mormons received more than one hundred thousand requests for these pamphlets.[16]

Like the spot of the Florida Council of Churches that encourages people to go to church, some religious PSAs have goals much more self-serving than those of the thought-provoking vignettes of the Episcopalians and the Franciscans and the public relations of the Mormons and the Nazarenes. In 1980, for example, the Reverend Mark Connolly produced seven spots (five in English and two in Spanish) with Foote, Cone, and Belding for $25,000. Their purpose was to recruit young men for the diocesan priesthood. One PSA began with a close-up of a young, handsome man who says, "I am twenty-eight years old. I comfort people who are ill. I counsel people who are mixed up. I touch a lot of lives. I give love. I get love in return." As the camera widens to show his liturgical collar, he says, "I've got the best job in the world." Broadcast at no cost by seventy-four television stations and more than two hundred radio stations, they elicited more than 1,700 responses in the mail.[17] Recently, the Missionary Oblates of Mary Immaculate used the same strategy for recruitment. However, instead of having a priest give his testimony, they used an actor, Don Novello. As Father Guido Sarducci on the comedy show "Saturday Night Live," he played the Vatican correspondent who encouraged viewers to "find the pope in the pizza."[18]

Producing religious PSAs, whether for evangelism, public relations, or recruitment, does not guarantee that they will be broadcast. For this reason, some organizations buy advertising time just as Rex Humbard, Pat Robertson, and Jimmy Swaggart do to promote their television ministries.[19] Because paid advertisements are guaranteed repetition at desirable times, those organizations that buy time believe that their spots will have a greater social impact.

Perhaps the most common type of paid religious advertising is what Larry Hollon of the National Council of Churches calls the "starving-baby syndrome." These ads, often made by relief agencies with religious affiliation, appeal for money to care for the starving and sick overseas. They often raise huge sums for relief, making their effectiveness beyond question. Unfortunately, they neglect the long-term problems of international economics and politics, imply that Third World cultures are inferior and dependent upon American largesse, and ignore the ways in which rich countries have contributed to Third World suffering. However pernicious their broader social meaning, fund-raising is an effective use of paid religious advertising.[20]

The effectiveness of paid advertising was the rationale behind the statewide public relations campaign and membership drive of the Baptist General Convention of Texas in the spring of 1977. Worried because the population of Texas was growing faster than the membership of the church, Texas Baptists designed Good News Texas, a campaign of evangelistic meetings in the local churches coordinated with $1.5 million worth of advertising. The centerpiece of the media campaign, called Living Proof, was a series of thirty-second prime-time television testimonials by celebrities who said that Jesus Christ solved their hopelessness, purposelessness, and lack of peace of mind.[21] The most memorable spot was a testimony by Eldridge Cleaver:

> Nobody ever believed in a philosophy stronger than I did. My name is Eldridge Cleaver. For 22 years I studied and practiced the communist ideology, until I finally had to leave this country because my life was in danger. Exile gave me a chance to see first hand the system I advocated. After 7 years in 15 countries, I found out that the philosophy I had faith in doesn't work in practice. The people I trusted don't even trust themselves. I didn't know who or what to believe anymore.
>
> Then I came face to face with a different kind of revolutionary. His name is Jesus Christ. Is he real? Can *he* be trusted to untangle a messed up world and a fouled up life?
>
> I'm living proof of it.[22]

The goal of Good News Texas was for every Texan to be "bombarded with the gospel message at least forty times during the campaign," thereby enhancing the image of the Baptist church and adding to its enrollment.[23]

The aims of the crusade, however, proved elusive. Every Texan did not see the spots; only about half did. Furthermore, instead of increasing enrollment, church additions fell 2.9 percent from the previous year, albeit less than the 10.1 percent decline in church additions that the Southern Baptist Convention as a whole experienced. The follow-up study admitted that "the primary function of the campaign was reinforcement, in that persons most often reached were those who already had some degree of religiosity." The study concluded by agreeing with a director of missions who said, "If one soul has been saved as a result of this, then every effort has been worth it all." Good News Texas was a public relations and recruiting failure.[24]

The Texas Baptists' failure has not stopped other organizations from using paid advertising for similar goals. In the fall of 1983, to celebrate the Year of the Bible, the Arthur S. DeMoss Foundation of Philadelphia paid between eight and ten million dollars to place short testimonials on television and in newspapers and magazines. The "Power for Living" campaign featured Pat Boone, Charles Colson, Tom Landry, and other celebrities who said that their relationship with God mattered most in their lives. Each ad offered a 130-page book, *Power for Living,* with "no strings attached." Over four million people called a toll-free number or sent in a coupon for the book.[25]

Given the diverse purposes for which religious PSAs and advertisements are produced, it is interesting to note the public's ambivalence and the clergy's acceptance of religious advertising. In 1985 Stephen W. McDaniel asked 551 persons throughout the United States, just over half of whom were clergy, to rank from inappropriate to appropriate advertising media that churches can use. They said that yellow-page ads, on-premise signs, and newspaper ads are the most appropriate advertising media for churches. They said that billboards, handbills, and such specialty ads as bumper stickers and pens are the least appropriate media. The clergy responded less conservatively to all forms of church advertising. For example, the public doubted the appropriateness of radio and television for churches, but the clergy judged them to be somewhat appropriate. The differences between clergy and the public extend beyond the use of media to the advertising of messages. McDaniel found that whereas clergy favor a broad range of advertising content, the public thinks that churches should not advertise their theological beliefs.[26]

Not only is there a difference between the way clergy and the general public feel about religious advertising, but there is a difference between the way churchgoers and nonchurchgoers feel about religious advertising. In a survey conducted for the American Lutheran Church, the firm Batten, Batten, Hudson & Schwab found that nonchurchgoers favored such advertising slightly more than churchgoers did.[27]

Nobody seems to object to church advertising by means of a community-events calendar, listing an upcoming event, touring musicians, or an annual barbecue. Cable systems and broadcast channels often operate this service free for nonprofit organizations. That no one complains about its use probably suggests that advertising an event is not controversial but that advertising an idea is.[28]

## Critics

Despite the benevolent intentions of the producers of religious advertisements and PSAs, there are those who argue that their enterprise is doomed from the start. They argue that producers' intentions are irrelevant because the medium is resistant to religion. These critics raise essential questions: Is television as a medium biased against religious communication, or is it a neutral medium that can broadcast both divine and demonic messages? Should religion be advertised at all?

These questions have already been answered in

England. Commercial television there is forbidden by the Independent Broadcasting Authority, its governing body, to advertise religion: "No advertisement may be inserted by or on behalf of any body, the objects of which are wholly or mainly of a religious nature, and no advertisement may be directed towards any religious end."[29] British authorities forbid opinion advertising, whether religious or political, because it is not available to everybody but only to those who can afford it.

In the United States, critics respond differently. Long before advertising on television became an avenue for religious expression, Reinhold Niebuhr scorned church advertising in newspapers. He believed that advertising could not meet the challenge of the Christian witness. His reasoning was partly sociological—those who used religious advertisements think less about communicating morality and spirituality than about capturing consumers and markets, gaining attention, and building attendance and conversion rates. Niebuhr also reasoned philosophically—advertisements are incapable of attesting to the personal and communal depths of religious life:

> If religion is a patented device that will magically solve the problems of life you can sell it, but if it is love of beauty and truth and righteousness you can not sell it at all. You can only stand ready to help those who are willing to adventure upon the difficult pilgrimage and to undergo the arduous discipline which finally brings them into the possession of life's highest spiritual values.[30]

According to Niebuhr, advertising is inappropriate for religious uses because it is a means of commercial expression, not of personal reflection or exhortation.

Virginia Stem Owens concurs with Niebuhr's judgments. She argues that television cannot be used for religious purposes, because it opposes Christianity. Religious television is not religious; it is a capitulation to the larger culture. "While we have been morally incensed at the contemporary slogan 'If it feels good, do it,' we have unconsciously adopted the equally reprehensible 'If it works, do it.' " Television projects images, says Owens, but true religion involves personal presence, something foreign to the medium of television. When "B. J. Thomas endorses Jesus as Bruce Jenner endorses cereal," television has replaced face-to-face interaction. Owens maintains that instead of spirituality, religious television communicates some distorted likeness, some surrogate.[31]

Malcolm Muggeridge argues similarly: "As a television performer, I see myself as a man playing a piano in a brothel, who includes 'Abide with Me' in his repertoire in the hope of thereby edifying both clients and inmates."[32] According to Muggeridge, television promotes fantasy, distracting viewers from the religious depths of human being. Likewise, Neil Postman says, "What makes . . . television preachers the enemy of religious experience is not so much *their* weaknesses but the weaknesses of the medium in which they work." Postman's thesis is that television makes all content, including religion, superficial. Unlike speech and writing, television lacks propositional content, so that it trivializes everything. On television, Christianity, which is demanding and serious, becomes easy and amusing: "The television screen wants you to remember that its imagery is always available for your amusement and pleasure."[33]

Superficiality is intrinsic to advertising, critics argue, because advertisements are necessarily short. Because their brevity does not permit the development of complex religious ideas, critics believe that opinion advertisements, political or religious, debase discussion rather than inform it.[34]

Advocates of the form retort that brief advertisements can be poignant and aesthetically ingenious. The brevity of the spots requires that they be repeated often if they are to have any impact at all. However, because free airtime is scarce, it is unlikely that individual PSAs will achieve the level of saturation they need to have some impact. Thus producers use different spots that focus on a single theme for several years.[35]

Those who argue that television undermines religious communication often base their objections on personality characteristics, as Niebuhr had. One early critic claimed that religious advertising on television "brings 'customers' into the church, not members; 'customers' in the sense that they have been sold something. These new church members are perhaps religious shoppers rather than people with a need for spiritual faith."[36] However, the objection to television on the grounds that television programmers and viewers think commercially rather than spiritually is little more than guilt by association. As A. William Bluem argued, there can be wheat among chaff, religious awareness despite crass commercialism:

> While some would object to the "marketing" of religion in this way, it is less than fair to condemn a *technique* which is successful and undoubtedly influential simply because it is also employed to elicit decisions to buy products and services. Brevity, the dramatic impact of conflict and resolution, genuinely creative graphic and cinematic technique, humor, taut and exciting structure—these are the vital elements of all successful art and communication, irrespective of the purpose served.[37]

In H. Richard Niebuhr's terms, the model to be followed is neither rejection, Christ against culture; nor accommodation, the Christ of culture; but rather change, Christ the transformer of culture.[38] Indeed, if spirituality is the best antidote to debasing commercialism, religious communicators are compelled to leaven television programming.

Unlike the objection to religious television based on personality, the argument that television is antireligious because it is an impersonal, one-way medium deserves more consideration. If true religion requires face-to-face dialogue, then television is clearly an unsuitable medium for religious communication. This argument must be evaluated on both its understanding of religion and its understanding of communications.

Ellens answers the naysayers on theological grounds. He claims that religious spots assume God's immanence:

> A spot is designed to startle a viewer or listener with an idea,
> question, or issue. That will force him to think seriously and
> thus experience some growth in Christian concern, under-
> standing, or action. The spot technique, therefore, assumes
> that the business of inciting humans to responsible godliness
> can be accomplished by confronting man with God's claim.
> That, in turn, assumes God to be immanent in his world—the
> world of man—and capable of confronting man, at least vi-
> cariously.[39]

The main problem with this claim is that its view of immanence is
limited. If God can awaken slumbering souls through religious
telespots, then God can also do so through any television show,
whether expressly religious or not. If religious spots can "provoke
unusually intense thought or feeling about a specific concern of
Christian behavior,"[40] as Ellens claims, then so can other PSAs, not
to mention television dramas and documentaries. However limited,
Ellens's view does clear room for the religious use of television, and
of commercial television spots in particular.

This concept of God's immanence underlies the Franciscans' production of telespots. In 1966 Franciscan Communications
of Los Angeles began producing PSAs with a Mother's Day spot,
which simply showed the faces of mothers of diverse races and
nationalities. The success of this pilot spurred them on so that by
1970 the Franciscans had some fifty religious spots produced by a
staff of twenty and funded with an annual budget of $150,000.[41]
They avoided being "overly religious" because of their assumption
that revealing the essentially human reveals the divine. According
to Tony Scannell, former president of the center, "We see a great
deal of religion in what others see as a human event."[42]

Not only do critics of religious broadcasting ignore the
idea of immanence, but their criterion of face-to-face immediacy
for religious communication is problematic. Critics denounce television for being a one-way medium, but they accept other mediated
communication channels that are just as unidirectional. Books,
including the Bible, are just such channels, but critics do not ques-

tion them. This inconsistency in their argument reveals a conservatism, a desire for the religious expression of a bygone era.

Is television as a medium biased against religious communication? Television is no more neutral than speech or print, as the Innis-McLuhan tradition has argued. At the turn of the century, Alfred Loisy understood that religion is not a static core of concepts that has weathered the assaults of history but is rather a set of dynamic, culturally conditioned responses springing from fundamental human needs expressed during different historical periods.[43] Religion during the oral era, when tribal wisdom was spoken and rehearsed through generations, is different from religion in the print era, when wisdom was recorded and codified and the tribes were splintered. In an age of electronically transmitted information, the nature of religious responses will surely change. In this respect, the answer to the question is yes. Television *is* biased against the logic of the religion of the print era.

But the answer must ultimately be no. The form and the content of religious responses will change, but responses will be religious nonetheless, because human beings will have spiritual needs and questions. To say that we should avoid television is to say that religion should stay the same—clearly a conservative fantasy. As there are better and worse books and better and worse sermons, there will be better and worse religious broadcasts.

However much this line of reasoning will inform our philosophies of history, it will not inform our immediate decisions concerning the religious use of television. We must ask a different set of questions.

## Gatekeepers

Television is not the neutral conduit that many religious broadcasters assume it to be. Its visual and temporal characteristics help shape the form of televised religious discourse. Nevertheless, television spots can be religious, even if they are influenced by the medium. However, as Dennis Benson discovered, producing television spots does not guarantee that stations will broadcast them: "One summer ten pastors in our area spent many days working on an experimental set of spots for a local television station. We wrote and produced five one-minute spots each. These were going to be used during the broadcast day. . . . We produced them, and they were never aired."[44] Had the ten pastors better understood the values of commercial broadcasters, they might not have so blithely assumed that stations would air whatever they received. Religious advertisers who are willing to pay for airtime can say virtually whatever the medium will allow. However, religious advertisers who want their spots to be broadcast as PSAs must adhere to the commercial biases of television gatekeepers.

A commercial medium that relies upon the attention of millions of viewers for its revenue will not broadcast advertisements that might offend the public. Thus all PSAs, whether for the Ad Council or for religious groups, are meek. Broadcasters select PSAs that are socially and politically safe.[45] According to Bluford Hestir, former director of Television, Radio, and Audio Visuals for the Southern Presbyterian church, "When we do not pay for the time, we are at the mercy of the station. We have to conform to the state of the art and the market."[46]

Potential controversy limited an otherwise popular series of spots in the 1960s distributed by the National Council of Churches. "Keep in circulation the rumor that God is alive" read the quilt being stitched by six women on one of the one-minute spots. According to Lois Anderson of the National Council of Churches, this series of spots meant "to stimulate thought and conversation about God. If later on people examine their faiths and decide to go to church, well, that's fine with us."[47] Although 230 stations in 119 cities ran the PSA, others rejected it as controversial. Edward R. Kenefick, then general manager of WBBM-TV in Chicago, asked, "What kind of position would I be in if someone came in the front door with a spot that said, 'Circulate the rumor that God is dead'?"[48]

To find out the gatekeeping criteria regarding religious PSAs more specifically, I mailed a questionnaire to program managers at 910 commercial television stations in the United States during the summer of 1987.[49] I received responses from 58 percent (525). Questions, both open-ended and closed-ended, concerned selection criteria and broadcast statistics. Responses were anonymous. When asked whether their stations sold time to religious broadcasters, 90.3 percent of program managers answered yes. However, only 78.7 percent of program managers said that their stations run religious PSAs. Clearly most commercial television stations program both paid and unpaid religious material. The difference in the percentages suggests that one out of five program managers prefers paid religious programming to unpaid religious programming.

The differing proportions of religious and nonreligious PSAs that television stations broadcast support this conclusion (see table 5.1). Although 68.6 percent of television stations run fewer than half of the religious PSAs they receive, only 46.6 percent run fewer than half of the nonreligious PSAs they receive. Program managers obviously prefer nonreligious PSAs to religious ones. One program manager wrote, "Religious groups have the money to buy advertising and if they wish to run PSAs, they may buy this time. Television time is very valuable and we would like to offer what little time is left to nonprofit local groups with real gripes." Another said bluntly, "We charge for all religious programs and spots." Program managers often disapprove of religious programming on commercial channels, but most of them will go ahead and program religious material despite their reservations if there is money to be made.

Historically, religious broadcasters have produced

**Table 5.1.   PSA preferences**

| Proportion of PSAs broadcast | Religious, % | Nonreligious, % |
|---|---|---|
| Less than one-fourth | 43.5 | 16.8 |
| One-fourth to one-half | 25.1 | 29.8 |
| One-half to three-fourths | 14.4 | 37.8 |
| Virtually all of them | 12.3 | 12.1 |
| No answer | 4.7 | 3.5 |

Note: $n = 423$.

twenty-, thirty-, and sixty-second spots. At least in theory, the sixty-second spot can develop an idea more fully than a twenty- or thirty-second spot, but the variety of lengths would help to ensure that the spots appeared at all. When asked what length PSAs their stations were most likely to broadcast, most program managers (70.4 percent) answered that they preferred thirty-second spots. Religious broadcasters no longer have the luxury of a minute to express their ideas; they have thirty seconds — that is, if they can get on the air at all.

When asked what most influenced their stations to broadcast religious PSAs, most program managers (41.4 percent) said the message (see table 5.2). Program managers had much to say about what they looked for in religious PSAs. One wrote, "Generally, spots are run if the message is 'good feeling' such as what the Church of the Latter Day Saints produces. We stay away from denominational spots that seem to recruit for their church or push a certain religious view." Another thought similarly: "We air only Church of the Latter Day Saints spots because they're beautifully produced and have excellent content and storyline and message." A third listed the values sought in religious PSAs: "We will help promote family values, a sharing spirit, a sense of stability in a troubled society, and hope." Program managers want uncontroversial moral universals.

**Table 5.2.** **Reasons for choosing religious PSAs as a function of market size**

|  | Top 100 markets, % ($n = 104$) | Remaining markets, % ($n = 148$) |
|---|---|---|
| Aesthetics | 11.5 | 12.5 |
| Message | 74.3 | 60.6 |
| Locality | 14.2 | 26.9 |

Note: Chi-square = 6.83, $p = .03$.

After the message, program managers ranked locality (11.6 percent) as the most important criterion for the selection of religious PSAs. Program managers in smaller markets are more concerned with localism than program managers in large markets are. One manager wrote, "Local PSAs or national PSAs with local end tags air more often than national PSAs due to an extra concern for our local community." A second said, "Any we turn down are most likely national sponsors which can't be localized to our coverage area." The emphasis on localism in smaller markets is probably due to the greater community allegiance in smaller cities.

Although station managers ranked aesthetics third (7.1 percent) among selection criteria, visual qualities do matter to them. One station manager complained, "Quite often, religious spots are not the slickest to watch. Many are thirty seconds filled by two or three poor quality slides with a phone number or a scripture passage." Another said, "I'd kill for genuinely humanistic and universal spots aimed at calming our world, *if they're of high quality visually*" (emphasis added). Program managers expect high aesthetic quality as a matter of course; they screen well-produced spots on the basis of the message.

To approach selection criteria another way, I asked station managers to name the last religious PSA that their stations rejected. Most answered that they rejected advertisements that had specific social or political appeals. "We are not a PTL station," said one, "yet we were asked to air an appeal for friends to save the PTL after the Bakker fiasco." The following list of rejected PSAs is illuminating: "a birth control PSA," "concerned Christians of pro-life issue — message and graphics not acceptable," "locally produced spot urging viewers to seek help for problems at specific church," "attend-church spot inviting viewers to a specific congregation," "a notice for a local revival," "something about nuclear armaments, because of political overtones," "touring gospel group to perform locally," "got overwhelmed with vacation Bible school announcements and stopped using them," and "one asking for donations."

This survey of television program managers documents two patterns regarding the broadcast of religious PSAs. First, most commercial television stations broadcast religious PSAs, but they reject as least half of those they receive. Second, to be accepted, religious PSAs should be superb, thirty-second productions with a universal moral appeal. In other words, to beat the fifty-fifty chance of acceptance, religious PSAs must be expensive, short, and politically bland.


## Conclusion

The incentive to use thirty-second television spots for religious purposes has grown since the 1960s, when free time for full-length religious programs began to decline steadily. The churches have responded in one of two ways. Some have chosen to guarantee airtime by purchasing advertising slots. Costs have run into the millions and the results have been ambiguous. Others have chosen to produce spots to be broadcast as PSAs. Costs have been much lower, but the messages have been necessarily timid.

Is either choice wise? That depends upon the rationale. Paid television spots are poor agents for proselytism and education because they are short and because television is a unidirectional, impersonal medium of communication. Proselytism and education through television are probably better achieved in regularly scheduled, full-length programming coordinated with personal interaction. Perhaps the best use of paid spots is for fund-raising. If cautiously used and sensitively written, broadcast advertisements can help raise funds for the disenfranchised.

The same conclusions apply to religious PSAs, with one major difference. Because they must gain the approval of commercial programmers, they must be inoffensive. Their noncontroversial nature alone makes them poor agents of proselytism and education, and fund-raising appeals will probably disqualify them as programmable PSAs. But they can be effective tools for internal public relations. Although PSAs are too brief and impersonal to change attitudes of people outside an organization, they can reinforce attitudes within an organization. Whether the Mormons have improved their image across the society is debatable, but they have surely promoted Mormon pride, which is an effective use of television spots.

    Fund-raising and internal public relations are uses far from the evangelical promise that early advocates of broadcast advertising believed television held. These modest uses are all that the commercial television industry presently offers to religious communicators. For purposes other than organizational, religious communicators will have to either invest heavily in regularly scheduled, full-length television programming or content themselves with writing and speaking.

# Religious Watchdog Groups and Prime-Time Programming

**MARK FACKLER**

Wilbur Schramm's celebrated text appeared over thirty years ago with a warning in its introduction by Reinhold Niebuhr, who by that time was in semiretirement, suffering the effects of a stroke, severe depression, and related illnesses. Niebuhr had served on the Commission on Freedom of the Press in 1947 and was an author of the so-called social responsibility theory of the press and an advocate of free and radical speech. He had praised the commission's call for greater public participation in mass media industries. Yet in Schramm's book he worried that a proliferation of public pressure groups "might reduce the mass entertainment industry to a new low of sentimentality and inanity. There is, in short, no easy way of forcing people to be responsible against their own inclination and beyond their capacity."[1] Today's  moral guardians of television programming would obviously take issue with Niebuhr's worry over proliferation and likely agree with him on the matter of "no easy way."

A recent exhibit at the New York Public Library carried the title "Censorship: 500 Years of Conflict." The numbers are significant. In a culture where one opinion dominates, where the technology of communication is controlled by exponents of the same, and where dissent is quiet on pain of fire or hellfire, censorship is unnecessary and conflict incidental. Obviously, since the day human speech first sounded, verbal disputes have challenged majority opinion and provoked censorial power.[2] But in the West, the era of the Reformation signaled the end of hegemony in its purist form. Five hundred years ago no systematic method existed to harness the flood of printed dissent. The power of the papal bull was put to ashes when Luther publicly burned *Contra Errores*. Since that time, a book condemned for its content was usually a most sought after book.[3]

In terms of modern mass media, the watchdog movement began the year after the first commercial film was shown in New York City. Wilbur Fisk Crafts established the International Reform Bureau in 1895 to lobby in Washington against drugs, alcohol, and motion pictures.[4] During the next three decades, civic and religious groups strenuously protested what they considered an exploitation of children and glorification of criminal and deviant behavior. When the Federal Motion Picture Council was organized in 1925, its program — "Nothing short of intervention by a centralized power outside the motion picture industry can bring about fundamental and permanent changes"[5] — was already the stated conviction of the Protestant Episcopal Church, the Methodist Episcopal General Conference, the Northern Baptist Convention, Worldwide Christian Endeavor, the General Assembly of the Presbyterian Church, and the Social Service Commission of the Federal Council of Churches. The Payne Fund studies put some muscle into legislation to create a national film review board, though that effort never succeeded.

While Protestants were organizing political support for an ultimately unsuccessful national forum, Catholics went to their membership with a program that, by its strength of numbers, did lead to structural adjustments in the pruning of objectionable content from motion pictures. On 11 April 1934, six months after a Vatican spokesman had called for a "united and vigorous" campaign to purify the cinema, nine million Catholics heard the 196-word pledge of the Legion of Decency and agreed to fight against "vile and unwholesome" pictures, to condemn "suggestive advertisements," and to "remain away" (the industry's nightmare) from films which offend "decency and Christian morality."

While many called the campaign censorship—Morris Ernst insisting that the censors had "flagellated life and courage from a promising craft"[6]—Catholics consistently framed the Legion's influence in terms of redemption, responsibility, and guardianship. Shunning the futile Protestant strategy, Catholic leadership assumed that churchly care of the creation required vigilance in the diet of entertainment its members consumed. "The Legion is not an appeal to state action," wrote *Commonweal* in late 1934, "but to the individual conscience."[7] The Legion's campaign was far more than mere consciousness-raising, of course; it was a concerted effort to use economic pressure against one of the nation's most profitable industries. Strengthened by Pope Pius XI's 1936 encyclical, *Vigilanti Cura,* the Legion and its supporters, which initially included several non-Catholic agencies, continued to influence movie content in the 1950s.

One might fully expect that fifty years of experience in watchdogging film would translate into a vigorous movement of television monitors already early in the 1950s, but such was not the case.[8] Religious guardians of television apparently found their raison d'être in the 1970 Report of the Commission on Obscenity and Pornography, the 1969 Report of the National Commission on the Causes and Prevention of Violence,[9] and the 1971 report of the Surgeon General's Scientific Advisory Committee on Television and Social Behavior.[10] From the dissenters of the 1970 report came Citizens for Decent Literature (now Citizens for Decency through Law) and new visibility to Morality in Media, founded in 1962. These reports themselves helped to inspire a belated, post–Vietnam era series of protests by religious organizations that has resulted in a bureaucratizing of the monitor movement and a standardizing of network and advertiser response.[11]

## The Road to CLeaR-TV

The story of television's religious watchdogs can be framed as a series of case studies wherein groups or individuals who were able to attract sufficient media attention succeeded in eliciting from targeted media companies certain concessions that the monitor group could use in claiming a victory for the moral campaign. Without some concession, Goliath triumphs over David and the campaign is lost. Without media attention, the monitor cannot claim to speak for the vast public beyond the immediate supporting constituency.[12]

The first notable case of a religious agency interacting effectively in television was the campaign of the Office of Communication of the United Church of Christ (UCC) against WLBT-TV in Jackson, Mississippi.[13] The story of the campaign is well known and ably told elsewhere.[14] The legacy of WLBT, however, was in the arena of federal regulation, the courts, and groups such as Action for Children's Television, the National Black Media Coalition, and the National Citizens Committee for Broadcasting, which do not represent specifically religious constituents and which do not frame their campaign in religious terms. Although several mainline denominations found inspiration from this midsixties context, this story does not include the highly charged religious metaphors that characterize the latter-day scenarios.

Following the courtroom denouement of WLBT,[15] the first wave of religiously framed monitors turned the focus away from racial bigotry and fairness in franchise licensing back toward the content-based issues that consumed earlier motion picture watchdog efforts. What was violence doing to children? What potentials of human development were being subverted or altogether missed by the mind-wasting television plug-in drug?

While the National Parent-Teacher Association (PTA) inaugurated a year-long program (1976) to address television violence and the American Medical Association resolved that television violence is "a risk factor threatening the health and welfare of young Americans,"[16] denominational agencies and synods struggled to frame their protests in language cleansed of theological references, yet saturated with moral potency. The results were un-spectacular. The United Methodist Church officially declared its opposition to censorship while declaring "that all communications must take place within a framework of social responsibility." The General Convention of the Episcopal Church would "protest against unacceptable displays of horror and cruelty in the media." The Lutheran Church–Missouri Synod resolved that "the exploita-tion of violence and sex in print, films, and stage productions is causing a sharp decline in moral standards." The Christian Church (Disciples of Christ) urged a reduction in "excessive and gratuitous violence on TV."[17]

     For obvious reasons such rhetoric as passed the general assemblies and synods of these major denominations posed little threat to network programmers. Who is to determine the threshold of "unacceptable displays"? Or who might outline a "framework of social responsibility"? Within such flexible calls to moral restraint, network programmers could easily manage their own rhetorical rejoinders. Moreover, these separate and relatively innocuous statements of protest had no organizational center, represented no concerted effort, posed no common threat. As long as denomina-tions, with their inbuilt suspicions and fragmented constituencies, conducted their campaigns as isolated and quasi-penitent voices, their cries might as well have been to a wilderness. The lesson of the Legion's power had not yet impressed itself on well-meaning Protestants.

     Rising beside the denominational protests, and ulti-mately their salvation, were broad-based coalitions of religiously motivated persons that put teeth into the protest movement. These coalitions focused complaints on specific programs and specific televised behaviors, produced semiempirical, quasi-observational data by which to measure both their grievances and network re-sponses, and threatened to use the ultimate weapon: the economic boycott. By abandoning the tradition of pulpit persuasion and adopting the appearance of bureaucratic efficiency—the epitome of which was network television itself—the monitors became legiti-mate actors in the drama. Almost by default, these independent groups began to develop public information campaigns, producing films and videos themselves, sponsoring workshops, and holding press conferences, all the media tricks of the industry they wished to change.

The mainstream monitors and the new economic pressure groups had their chance in 1977 to test tactics against each other as much as against their common foe. The target was "SOAP," a new ABC sitcom that programming chief Fred Silverman claimed was just an "innovative form of character comedy." Actually the drama was to include a wealthy lecher, an impotent blue-collar worker, and sons and daughters in various scrapes, from Mafia membership to a nunnery. There would be humorous racism and silly transvestism. The idea seemed so far ahead of contemporary television comedy that even local stations, after pre-screening, were calling it "one long dirty joke . . . bad for television."[18]

Reaction from the mainstream included a condemnation by the U.S. Catholic Conference ("a new debasement of the medium through a contempt for human beings")[19] and the UCC ("the opening wedge for sexually explicit material in prime-time").[20] The National Council of Catholic Bishops joined the UCC, the United Methodist Church, and the National Council of Churches in urging local stations to honor community interests over network profits.[21] While this ad hoc coalition claimed to represent 138,000 local churches, it actually represented only four church organizations against one massive full-steam-ahead ratings-hungry network. And Fred Silverman was not a person to be out-argued. As the press began to report the coalition's call to arms, Silverman defended the sitcom's concept as "an intelligent show written and produced by intelligent people, and in time it will be perceived as a moral show."[22]

Augmenting the coalition's anger over "SOAP," several groups in 1977 began to rally constituents against prime-time abuses. The Southern Baptist Convention issued a package of materials called "Help for TV Viewers" that urged viewer involvement with the medium to include the boycott of products advertised on objectionable programs. But the consumer action was to be local, even individual. The Knights of Columbus Supreme Council called for persuasive tactics against networks, then boycotts if necessary. Also in 1977 the Telecommunications Consumer Coalition (TCC) was formed by the UCC, Consumers Union, and the Consumer Federation of America. The TCC would become a major clearinghouse for denominations and also for the National PTA, Union of American Hebrew Congregations, Black Citizens for Fair Media, and about 125 other participants. Coalitions were growing, expertise was in place, spokespeople were assembling, but still without the kind of telling pressure that reaches to the sunlit floors of New York's network fiefdom.

Then another kind of pressure group appeared, like the cloud on the horizon as small as a man's hand: grassroots southern activism unencumbered by New England civility. The new federation believed it was the rain in a drought-parched land and entered the battle with the fervor of Elijah on Mount Carmel. The first formal action of preacher Donald Wildmon's National Federation for Decency (NFD) was a "Turn the TV Off" week in the spring of 1977. Wildmon was a Methodist minister in Southaven, Mississippi, a suburb of Memphis, when he urged his congregation to turn off their sets. The idea became a bandwagon campaign, and as a result, the NFD, recently renamed the American Family Association (AFA), was born. Did Wildmon actually convince a million viewers to commit themselves to the ultimate boycott? Reports began to claim as much, and such reports tend to create a reality that takes on a life of its own.[23] Like the cloud on Elijah's horizon, NFD's first effort signified growing power and prominence.

Donald Wildmon began his career as a circuit preacher out of Iuka, Mississippi. He spent eight years at Lee Acres Methodist Church in Tupelo before moving to Southaven. A part-time sportswriter and author, he charts his course into media activism from efforts during the Christmas holidays of 1976 to find network programming suitable for family viewing.

Encouraged by the response to the No-TV week, Wildmon resigned the Southaven church, moved back to Tupelo, and started the NFD in early 1977, underwriting costs with his own savings. The NFD joined in the summer protests of "SOAP" and credits itself with causing more than 32,000 letters of protest to be written against that show.[24]

The "SOAP" protests actually drew together an unusual coalition of religious groups, from the Southern Baptist Christian Life Commission (which led the protests) to the U.S. Catholic Conference. The *Texas Methodist, Texas Catholic,* and *Baptist Standard* published a joint editorial criticizing the program. All three groups were also represented at church rallies in Texas. Meanwhile, the Church of God (Cleveland, Tennessee) polled 175,000 families, who rated "SOAP" as the second most offensive show on the air ("Maude" won the poll), and the Reverend Jerry Falwell's 375,000-member poll called "SOAP" the worst program on television.[25] Even the liberal *Commonweal* protested the program as "dirty-minded," and *Newsweek* concluded its summary of future "SOAP" scripts by saying that "absolutely nothing is 'too weird' for ABC — as long as the ratings are right."[26]

Although momentum seemed to ebb for the religious monitors as the "me" decade turned into the 1980s, Wildmon and the NFD had learned a valuable lesson: in coalition is thy strength. The NFD claimed credit for persuading Sears to drop sponsorship of "Three's Company" and "Charlie's Angels" in 1978, but the time had come for new strategies and broader agendas.

The second phase of Wildmon's efforts began three months after the election of Ronald Reagan with the appearance of the National Coalition for Better Television (NCBT), a cooperative effort of more than 150 organizations which represented perhaps five million viewers. The NCBT was a limited partnership between the NFD and the Reverend Jerry Falwell's amazingly successful Moral Majority, with other conservative groups coming along for the journey; Phyllis Schlafly of The Eagle Forum sat on the NCBT board.

The scale of operation was escalating. NCBT claimed to have up to 450,000 monitors (only 4,000 actually took part), working in groups of two, watching three months of programming in the spring of 1981. The goal of this massive effort was to isolate one or two sponsors of "gratuitous sex and violence" and to call upon NCBT member agencies to urge constituents into a one-year moratorium on the purchase of dry goods marketed by the guilty sponsor.[27] The boycott would have been heartrending for typical American families, given the wide range of products involved, but offending sponsors made peace at a Memphis meeting with Wildmon in late June. Procter & Gamble Company, for example, agreed to withdraw backing from more than fifty shows. Procter and Gamble chairman Owen B. Butler lent legitimacy to the coalition in a surprisingly supportive statement made to the Academy of Television Arts and Sciences in Los Angeles: "We think the Coalition for Better Television is expressing some very important and broadly held views. . . . I can assure you that we are listening very carefully to what they say."[28] *Newsweek* called Wildmon the "ayatollah of the airwaves," yet the Mississippi preacher was now testifying before congressional subcommittees and debating network presidents on the "Phil Donahue Show."

Then in March 1982 the NCBT announced a boycott of RCA and NBC.[29] All the promises of change made in Memphis nine months earlier had not changed TV programming, the NFD monitors determined that fall. RCA owned the NBC network, but all the products of RCA (rental cars, carpeting, and other nonmedia goods) were targeted. Mainline denominations withheld support, believing that the NCBT was solely a coalition of the New Right; perhaps they were also reluctant to help a religious group whose primary method of influencing broadcasting was the boycott. Nonetheless, in December 1982 Wildmon claimed that the boycott was going "extremely well," although RCA responded that corporate earnings were up 75 percent.[30] Intoned Gene Jankowski of CBS, "We are now faced with an organized attempt . . . an unprecedented usurpation of the individual viewer's right of choice and a direct assault on the creative community's freedom of enterprise. It is an attempt at prior restraint on a grand scale."[31]

The third stage of Wildmon's movement portends even greater clout, a more potent constituency, and the building of even broader coalitions. Yet its effectiveness is matched by network and sponsor conciliation that may diffuse NFD's rhetoric and limit any real gains.

In December 1985 Wildmon and Billy Melvin, head of the National Association of Evangelicals, a loosely held together umbrella agency for several fiercely independent conservative denominations, called together two dozen leaders of denominations, mission agencies, and religious colleges for a strategy meeting at O'Hare Airport in Chicago. They were part of a group of seventeen hundred signees of a "Statement of Concern" developed by Wildmon and Melvin earlier that year and submitted to three thousand heads of Christian agencies and schools. No specific television program gave incentive to this meeting but rather the growing presence of the four NFD-defined problem areas: sex, violence, profanity, and anti-Christian stereotyping in news and entertainment programming.

Data that served as the basis for the concerns expressed in Chicago came from NFD monitors: one thousand viewers organized into twenty-five to thirty teams, who watch all prime-time nonpolitical programming, including sports, and report their findings to NFD headquarters in Tupelo, where a staff throws out high scores and low scores and compiles the rest. The team of monitors changes every month, Wildmon claims, and the purpose of all the data collection is to rate sponsors as well as programs.[32]

From the initial meeting at O'Hare came an executive board of a new coalition called CLeaR-TV, for Christian Leaders for Responsible Television. Wildmon was appointed executive director; Melvin was appointed chair of the executive board. Expenses and hierarchies were to be kept as small as possible, these leaders determined, and CLeaR-TV was to grow as large as possible, at least in terms of the constituencies represented by the signees of the "Statement of Concern."

The "Statement of Concern" is a remarkably clear document recognizing television's power and appealing for television's reformation. The document admits that "Christians have no monopoly on virtue" and shares concerns with "people of all beliefs"

who embrace the values of faithfulness, kindness, and honesty—
quite an admission for a fundamentalist movement, but apparently
the NFD and the National Association of Evangelicals have broken
with old rhetorics of separatism and exclusivity. The document
places major responsibility for reducing violence with network
chiefs and broadcast licensees, though the subsequent campaign by
CLeaR-TV would be directed against advertisers. The document
states that NFD ratings results show 9.82 "sex incidents" per hour
and a 100 percent increase in the use of profane language from
1978 to 1984. The document calls upon networks and advertisers to
"take immediate steps to reduce incidents of sex and violence and
profanity" by 35 percent by the fall of 1987. In addition, the document calls for an immediate end to anti-Christian stereotyping,
which means that "Christians should be treated in a fair and un-
biased manner, as should all other religions"—which essentially
extends the antistereotyping mandate to cover all faiths. Finally,
the document assures the commercial television industry that
CLeaR-TV "will not go away." The calls to reform are made in
earnest; energy to monitor the networks' compliance is abundant.
The list of signees to the statement included Lutherans, Pentecostals, Baptists, and Catholics (including archbishops of Chicago,
Boston, Los Angeles, San Francisco, Miami, and New Orleans).
No funds were requested from any of these agencies or persons,
and no appeal was made for lay members. The NFD staff handles
clerical duties for CLeaR-TV, and NFD covers postage. The only
monetary obligation of member agencies is travel costs.

Those occasional travel expenses did play a brief role in
CLeaR-TV strategy in April 1986. Early that month the CLeaR-TV
executive board met with the three network standards chiefs in
New York to present the "Statement of Concern" and supporting
data. What occurred at those meetings, as best we can know it,
reflects the radically different frames of reference each group lives
in.

From the CLeaR-TV side, the meetings in New York
were symbolic only. Evidence presented to network personnel did
not seem to coax them toward change, nor did the discussions

appear to be anything more than polite public relations. One board executive summarized the perception of CLeaR-TV representatives:

1. The networks were all opposed to any monitoring system that tends to quantify program content.
2. None of the networks would admit to television as an educational tool. Entertainment was the goal, not education.
3. In reply to specific charges, networks claimed they represented a mosaic of American life.
4. Response from network representatives was so uniform that one could assume they "ate lunch together" and were voicing a common response to outside troublemakers.[33]

Officially, the executive board told the CLeaR-TV members that "none of the networks agreed to our request [to reduce violence, sex, profanity, and stereotyping by 35 percent] and none of the three gave any indication that they would make any changes in their programming."[34] CLeaR felt its petitions had fallen on deaf ears and worried that the petitions had not been received by people willing to listen to evidence or positioned to effect change.

The networks perceived the meetings as cordial, dialogical, informative, and part of ongoing efforts to keep abreast of public taste and preference. Network representatives had come to talk, and talk they did. The agenda from their point of view was fulfilled, and the stage set for further mutually helpful discussions.[35]

CLeaR-TV, however, was not about to wait for further conversation with the networks. Two weeks after the New York trip, the executive board met in Chicago and invited four chief commercial sponsors of objectionable television to discuss their advertising policies. Of the four, only Warner-Lambert came to CLeaR-TV; Miles Labs, Wendy's, and American Motors either made no response or declined to meet. Again, CLeaR-TV seemed unable to move decision makers toward change.

Next, the board determined that renewed NFD monitoring efforts in the fall of 1986 would reveal whether anyone had taken the call for a 35 percent reduction seriously. If not, a couple of sponsors would be singled out for boycott action. Finally, in July 1987 CLeaR-TV announced boycotts against Mazda Motors and the Noxell Corporation. Constituents were told that "Mazda has ignored all communications from CLeaR-TV, and is the leading sponsor of sex, violence and profanity incidents . . . for the last five years cumulatively," and Noxell "has shown a 70% increase in its sponsorship of offensive material from 1981–86."[36] Noxell quickly responded and the boycott threat was lifted. Mazda, however, appeared truculent.

Wildmon admitted that it is difficult to boycott a manufacturer of cars and trucks,[37] but when asked whether a mere letter of intent toward goodwill would be sufficient to lift the boycott, he indicated that only the promise of substantive change would do. Apparently that promise was forthcoming as the boycott went into the fall car-buying season, for in October CLeaR-TV reported that Mazda had assured them that "specific steps would be taken . . . to resolve the problem."[38] To keep the campaign alive, CLeaR-TV began correspondence with thirteen unnamed companies about their sponsorship of sex, violence, and profanity.

The boycott was purely symbolic. Consumers were provided with none of the data, were given only the most cursory reports of Noxell and Mazda compliance, and were never told what gains to expect on home television screens for their cooperation in the boycott. In fact, consumers were irrelevant to this boycott— nearly as irrelevant as real viewers are to the NFD-CLeaR strategy to clean up television. What mattered in this "consumer effort" was press release and printed notice, just as what matters in NFD data are collected reports, not viewer preferences. It was and is a campaign of rhetoric only.

## The Rhetorical Conflict

Industry response to pressure groups has always run the gamut from claims of censorship, expressed in a rhetorical style akin to Fred Friendly's telling phrase "killing gnats with a sledge hammer," to the mild-mannered accommodation of such groups as pests to be defanged through dialogue. When CBS president Thomas Wyman claimed in 1981 that the NCBT and Moral Majority "strike at the very heart of the American ideal of a free market-place," he allied himself with the free speech tradition that Wildmon also employed to explain his agenda. To sympathetic right-of-center readers of *Religious Broadcasting,* Wildmon wrote in 1982: "Here is our premise: The networks can show what they desire to show; the advertiser can sponsor what he desires to sponsor; the viewer can watch any of the options made available to him by the networks; . . . and the consumer can spend his money where he desires. For following that pure rule of democratic capitalism the networks compare me with Hitler, McCarthy, and Ayatollah Khomeini."[39]

Wildmon has effectively used the generic "great struggle" metaphor to rally supporters, warning that modernists wish to subvert the Judeo-Christian foundation of the United States, which admittedly has not rendered the perfect social order, "but it has been the most perfect system ever devised in the history of mankind. . . . We are caught up in our country today in a great struggle unlike any which we have faced before. Our struggle is not with an enemy from beyond our shores. . . . This great struggle . . . is going on inside our borders."[40]

But the struggle Wildmon exhorts us to join is closer yet, not only within our borders (lots of undesirable elements coexist within national borders) but also within the very heart and soul of the family and the church, in figure at least. For the Protestant, the pulpit is the central symbol of authority. On the pulpit the Bible lies open; from the pulpit sermons teach the revelation of God; from the pulpit prayers ascend. Thus when Wildmon warns supporters that television is the modern pulpit, that television programs are preachments in every way like the weekly gathering of the church, and that the revelation of these network sermons is the good news of secular humanism, he has touched a sacred symbol and suggested a most intolerable invasion, as if Nebuchadnezzar were again dismantling the ancient Temple, indeed as if the Abomination of Desolation were already within the Temple courts (Daniel 9:27).[41]

On the other side, network response is often soft-toned and impassive. In reply to my queries regarding network response to Wildmon's most recent campaign, all three public relations chiefs responded promptly that their efforts to meet with CLeaR-TV leaders and their own concern for broadcast standards are genuine. None of the responses advanced accusations, and none employed the metaphor of struggle. Rather, all three responses insisted that dialogue was the touchstone, that "listening and understanding" was the only network tactic. They all stopped short of articulating any agreement with the monitor's aims, and CBS especially expressed disappointment that the network's only feedback from CLeaR-TV since the New York meetings had been through press conferences that had distorted the nature of the meetings.[42] ABC has strategically employed a published content analysis that suggests most television drama is resolved within a Judeo-Christian framework of values. Especially helpful to the network position is the study's conclusion: "Television script writers rarely stray from a few narrow themes that have been espoused by mainstream religious cultures. . . . In a subtle way, without explicitly articulating religious doctrine, prime-time television programs incorporated the principles that have, over time, served the church."[43]

## The Monitors as Mentors

Yet assessing the monitor groups is not a simple matter of taking census, quoting studies, and compiling "statements of concern." At work in the watchdog function is a profound human need to keep order, to make order, to struggle against what Christians call carnality and Freudians call the id. Arthur Schlesinger,

Jr., no friend of censors, observes that "the instinct to suppress
. . . is rooted above all in profound human propensities to faith
and to fear."[44] I am not convinced that fear motivates the television
monitors as much as religious faith and fervor. The faith defines
reality; the fervor makes abstractions come to life in the context of
social struggle. Certainly the monitors use fear to heat up the
boilers of the less fervent. Yet the issue, in whatever mix of fear
and faith, goes beyond the sociology of economics and even beyond the normal interests of theological ethics. The monitor movement has a missiological impulse akin to the most ancient cries of
the Judeo-Christian scriptures to "subdue the earth" and to "have
dominion over every living thing that moveth upon the earth"
(Genesis 1:28). Humans are responsible under the Creator for the
world's care. The monitors extend that caretaking role beyond the
beasts and fowl of the Genesis story to their celluloid and video-
taped images. If that is too precarious a leap, it does not seem so to
them. They are stewards of the symbolic world as surely as their
forebears were gardeners, hunters, and inventors of tools and shel-
ter. The monitors' conviction that the symbolic world is the real
arena of struggle today is not so much a revival of the fanaticism
of "the old supernatural religions" (Schlesinger's dismissive comment)[45] as the normal response of the faithful to the task of tending
the created order.

From Walter Lippmann to Jacques Ellul, we have been
warned about the power of symbol to generate public mispercep-
tion, indeed about the near impossibility of educating a public
about the world as it really is without the distorting influence of
bias and ideology. From Frederic Wertham to Stuart Hall, we have
learned the impact of modern visual media—their subtle influence
on beliefs and latent influence on behavior. Certainly none of the
three major players in this drama—networks, advertisers, and
monitors—has failed to observe these modern commonplaces or to
understand their pivotal role in the making of the symbolic universe. Television, if not the altar of popular religion, is surely the
purveyor of the culture's common narratives. Network disclaimers
about "mere entertainment" are no more convincing than adver-

tiser disclaimers about buying demographics and not content. All players bear responsibility, though usually only the monitors acknowledge responsibility in forthright moral terms. Our question is whether the monitors are gadflies or legitimate members of the cast.

The rationale for intermediaries between the individual and the state finds its major voice in Tocqueville, but those sentiments are echoed and reissued with near cyclical regularity. C. Wright Mills, no advocate of churchly concerns, lamented the decline of voluntary associations as "genuine instruments of the public" and called vigorously for a rebirth of "intermediate associations" to negotiate the interests of family and small community against larger bureaucracies.[46] Ellul has called this process of authenticating group values a key to cultural survival.[47] Robert Bellah concludes that American individualism in the 1980s has grown cancerous, overwhelming those social integuments that alleviate modernity's destructive potentialities. Against the egalitarian love ethic, which provides no basis whatever for self-sacrifice, and the clipped television dialogue interrupted by incoherent commercial messages, Bellah advocates a return to values based on the long-standing traditions of groups which proffer norms for personal and social ethics.[48] The call to normativity grounded in the true narrative of groups living authentically is the heart of Stanley Hauerwas's recent contributions.[49]

If voluntary associations are indeed the primary units of responsible social change, the legitimacy of the role of monitors is self-evident. Democratic pluralism gives space to them; participatory democracy mandates their voice and influence. Without the monitors, the viewer stands essentially powerless against network bureaucracy. Although it may stretch the metaphor, no drama succeeds without a credible antagonist, and the antagonism of the monitors stands firmly in the tradition of Montesquieu, Milton, Jefferson, Madison, Lippmann, the woebegone Hutchins Commission of 1947, and the vast untamed school of media ethics called social responsibility theory, all parties that knew that the rights and responsibilities of symbol-making turn on the notion of virtue-bound liberty—not marketplace *caveat emptor* and not top-down Theory X management of information.[50]

The monitor movement also stands in the tradition of H. Richard Niebuhr's enduring schema Christ and culture in paradox.[51] The monitors make no pretense of converting the networks and Christianizing the media—no call for a television menu of mass revival meetings or coffee-cake Bible studies. Theirs is the task of retardation, halting the flow of moral laxity by taking the contest into the economic arena, where the stakes are profit and loss, where winners and losers can measure their strength against the common currency of the bottom line. Perhaps the rhetoric of struggle so necessary to winning and keeping financial support compels the monitors toward this adversarial model; perhaps their sense that the virtues they represent are so completely lacking advocates within the television hierarchy also makes "paradox" the most prudential posture.

Will reduced network power—the diversification of cable channels, the democratization of community-originated programs, the tiresome repetition of network television's ritual plots and settings—eventually lead the monitor movement from antagonism toward the peak of Niebuhr's pentagon, Christ the transformer of culture? To hope it will is to say that the world of symbol and culture is integral to that great narrative beginning in the expulsion of Genesis and concluding in the redemption of the Apocalypse. In the interim, however, the monitor movement, for all its rhetorical imprecision and myopic campaigning, is witness to the persistence of moral conscience and group solidarity that the Christian vision explains and that democratic governance protects.

# NOTES

## Introduction

1. Edward Bellamy, *Looking Backward: 2000–1887* (1888; reprint, New York: Penguin Books, 1986), p. 194.

2. Raymond Williams, *Communications,* 3d ed. (Harmondsworth: Penguin Books, 1976), p. 133.

3. Virginia Stem Owens, *The Total Image, or Selling Jesus in the Modern Age* (Grand Rapids, Mich.: William B. Eerdmans, 1980).

4. Edward J. Carnell, *Television: Servant or Master?* (Grand Rapids, Mich.: William B. Eerdmans, 1950).

5. Gregor T. Goethals, *The TV Ritual: Worship at the Video Altar* (Boston: Beacon, 1981).

6. Frederick Ferré, *Basic Modern Philosophy of Religion* (New York: Charles Scribner's Sons, 1967), p. 69.

7. John Wiley Nelson, *Your God Is Alive and Well and Appearing in Popular Culture* (Philadelphia: Westminster Press, 1976).

8. Sydney W. Head and Christopher H. Sterling, *Broadcasting in America: A Survey of Television, Radio, and New Technologies,* 4th ed. (Boston: Houghton Mifflin, 1982), p. 391.

## 1: Television Drama as a Sacred Text

1. Jean Shepherd, *A Fistful of Fig Newtons* (New York: Doubleday, 1981), p. 162.

2. Stanley Hauerwas, "Story and Theology," *Religion in Life* 45 (Autumn 1976): 343.

3. Johann Baptist Metz, "A Short Apology of Narrative," in Johann Baptist Metz and Jean-Pierre Jossua, eds., *The Crisis of Religious Language* (New York: Herder & Herder, 1973), p. 86.

4. Quoted in ibid., p. 86.

5. Ibid., p. 95.

6. Hannah Arendt, *The Human Condition* (Chicago: Univ. of Chicago Press, 1958), p. 181.

7. Quoted in Hauerwas, "Story and Theology," p. 348.

8. William Stringfellow, *A Simplicity of Faith* (Nashville: Abingdon, 1982), p. 20.

9. Ronald C. Arnett, *Communication and Community* (Carbondale: Southern Illinois Univ. Press, 1986), pp. 124, 125.

10. See, e.g., Horace Newcomb, ed., *Television: The Critical View*, 4th ed. (New York: Oxford Univ. Press, 1987); E. Ann Kaplan, ed., *Regarding Television: Critical Approaches—An Anthology* (Frederick, Md.: University Publications of America, 1983); John Fiske and John Hartley, *Reading Television* (London: Methuen, 1978); Todd Gitlin, ed., *Watching Television* (New York: Pantheon, 1986).

11. I suggest three reasons for this. First, much television criticism is frequently done by people who like to watch a lot of television rather than study television. Second, art criticism in general today is under the shadow of modern subjectivism, which holds that there really are no standards for criticism; one critic's views are as "accurate" as any other critic's views. Third, the field of communication produces many researchers who are methodologically sophisticated but theoretically uneducated.

12. See, e.g., Walter R. Fisher, *Human Communication as Narration: Toward a Philosophy of Reason, Value, and Action* (Columbia: Univ. of South Carolina Press, 1987).

13. Many of these historical developments are addressed in a special issue of the *Journal of Communication,* 33 (Summer 1983), entitled *Ferment in the Field.*

14. This is discussed cogently in Raymond Williams, "On High and Popular Culture," *New Republic,* 23 November 1974, pp. 13–16.

15. David Thorburn, "Television as an Aesthetic Medium," *Critical Studies in Mass Communication* 4 (June 1987): 161–62.

16. Nicholas Wolterstorff, *Art in Action* (Grand Rapids, Mich.: William B. Eerdmans, 1980), p. 144.

17. Hugh Dalziel Duncan, *Language and Literature in Society* (New York: Bedminster Press, 1953).

18. Quoted in Metz, "A Short Apology of Narrative," p. 86.

19. Wesley A. Kort, *Narrative Elements and Religious Meanings* (Philadelphia: Fortress Press, 1975), p. 5.

20. James W. Carey, "A Cultural Approach to Communication," *Communication* 2 (1975): 1–22.

21. Stanley Hauerwas, *Vision and Virtue* (Notre Dame, Ind.: Fides Publishers, 1974), pp. 71, 74.

22. Martin Esslin, *The Age of Television* (San Francisco: Freeman, 1982), p. 44.

23. I have discussed this at some length in "Popular Culture

and Life-Style Politics," *Journal of Communication Inquiry* 6 (Spring 1981): 87–96.

24. John Narone, *The Jesus Story: Our Life as Story in Christ* (Collegeville, Minn.: Liturgical Press, 1979), p. 71.

25. Sallie TeSelle, "The Experience of Coming to Belief," *Theology Today* 22 (July 1975): 160.

26. Tom Diver, *Patterns of Grace* (San Francisco: Harper & Row, 1977), p. 118.

27. The producer probably maintains the most control over the production process. See, e.g., Horace Newcomb and Robert S. Alley, *The Producer's Medium* (New York: Oxford Univ. Press, 1983). However, power and resources are still dispersed, though unequally, among many different people and organizations. See Joseph Turow, *Media Industries: The Production of News and Entertainment* (New York: Longman, 1984).

28. Among the more interesting attempts are Benjamin Stein, *The View from Sunset Boulevard* (Garden City, N.Y.: Doubleday, Anchor Books, 1980); and S. Robert Lichter, Stanley Rothman, and Linda S. Lichter, *The Media Elite* (Bethesda, Md.: Adler & Adler, 1986).

29. Wesley A. Kort, *Modern Fiction and Human Time* (Tampa: Univ. of South Florida Press, 1985), p. 13.

30. Wolterstorff, *Art in Action,* pp. 34–44.

31. Fisher, *Human Communication as Narration,* p. 87.

32. Julian N. Hartt, *A Christian Critique of American Culture* (New York: Harper & Row, 1967), pp. 405–6.

33. Louis Wirth, *On Cities and Social Life* (Chicago: Univ. of Chicago Press, 1964), pp. 19–20.

## 2: Religion on Television

1. Nick Browne, "The Political Economy of the Television (Super) Text," *Quarterly Review of Film Studies* 9 (Summer 1984): 174.

2. Todd Gitlin, ed., *Watching Television* (New York: Pantheon, 1986).

3. Horace Newcomb, "On the Dialogic Aspects of Mass Communication," *Critical Studies in Mass Communication* 1 (March 1984): 34–50.

4. John Fiske, "Television: Polysemy and Popularity," *Critical Studies in Mass Communication* 3 (December 1986): 391–408; Tamar Liebes, "Ethnocriticism: Israelis of Morrocan Ethnicity Negotiate the Meaning of 'Dallas' " *Studies in Visual Communication* 10 (1984): 46–72; Elihu Katz and Tamar Liebes, "Once upon a Time in 'Dallas,' " *Intermedia* 12 (May 1984): 28–32; R. Hodge and D. Tripp, *The Active Eye* (London: Polity Press, 1987); D. Morley, *Family Television* (London: Comedia, 1987).

5. Andrew Greeley, "Today's Morality Play: The Sitcom,"

*New York Times,* 17 May 1987, Arts and Leisure section, p. 40.

6. Clifford G. Christians, "The Sensate in Sorokin and in Primetime Television," *Et Cetera* 38 (Summer 1981): 195, 196.

7. Paul Schrader, *Transcendental Style in Film: Ozu, Bresson, Dreyer* (Los Angeles: Univ. of California Press, 1972).

8. Christians, "The Sensate in Sorokin and in Primetime Television," p. 197.

9. Greeley, "Today's Morality Play," p. 40.

10. Peter Brooks, *The Melodramatic Imagination: Balzac, Henry James, Melodrama, and the Mode of Excess* (New Haven: Yale Univ. Press, 1976).

11. Umberto Eco, "Innovation and Repetition: Between Modern and Post-Modern Aesthetics," *Daedalus* 114 (Fall 1985): 180.

## 3: Television and Public Virtue

1. All quotes attributed to persons in the television industry are from interviews conducted by me and, since 1977, by my partner Professor Irby B. Brown.

## 4: Network News Coverage of Religion

1. David G. Bromley and Anson D. Shupe, Jr., *America: Cult, Church, and Crusade* (Beverly Hills, Calif.: Sage, 1979), pp. 19–22; John Brice, "Guiding Lights," *Public Relations Journal* 42 (January 1986): 20–25; Jane Rothschild, "Training Journalists for Jesus," *Washington Journalism Review,* April 1986, pp. 45–47; Joseph Ferullo, "Flacking in the Fields of the Lord," *Channels,* March 1987, pp. 45–48.

2. James Davison Hunter, *American Evangelism: Conservative Religion and the Quandary of Modernity* (New Brunswick, N.J.: Rutgers Univ. Press, 1983), pp. 11–17; Albert Kreiling, "Television in American Ideological Hopes and Fears," pp. 39–57, and Horace M. Newcomb and Paul M. Hirsch, "Television as a Cultural Forum: Implications for Research," pp. 58–73, in Willard D. Rowland, Jr., and Bruce Watkins, eds., *Interpreting Television: Current Research Perspectives* (Beverly Hills, Calif.: Sage, 1984); Judith M. Buddenbaum, Survey of Religion News Editors and Writers: Summary of Findings (Geneva: Lutheran World Federation, 1982), p. 7; Judith M. Buddenbaum, "News about Religion: A Readership Study," *Newspaper Research Journal* 3 (January 1982): pp. 7–17.

3. Kreiling, "Television in American Ideological Hopes and Fears," pp. 53–54; Hunter, *American Evangelism,* pp. 7–9, 17–19; Buddenbaum, Survey, p. 8.

4. Elmo Roper, *Changing Public Attitudes toward Televi-*

*sion and Other Media* (New York: Roper Organization, 1983).

     5. Michael J. Robinson, "Reflections on the Nightly News," in Richard P. Adler, ed., *Understanding Television* (New York: Praeger, 1981), pp. 313–64.

     6. Ibid., pp. 322–28, 337–40; Hunter, *American Evangelism,* pp. 49–60.

     7. "No News Is Bad News," *Denver Post,* 15 March 1986, p. 14F; see also John M. Kraps, "Press Coverage of Religion: Better, but Not Good Enough," *Christian Century,* 5 November 1986, pp. 978–79; "Reporting Religion," *America,* 28 January 1984, p. 43; "The Challenge of Faithful Reporting," *Sojourners,* April 1979, pp. 21–22, 24.

     8. Cal Thomas, "Not Ready for Prime-Time Prayers," *Quill,* October 1986, pp. 15–19; see also Donald E. Wildmon, "Let's Get Religion in the Picture," *Christianity Today,* 19 February 1982, p. 11; "Bias beyond Understanding," ibid., 18 September 1981, pp. 13–14.

     9. William Fodiak, "How the Catholic Clergy in Pennsylvania Views the Media," *Editor & Publisher,* 27 December 1986, pp. 25, 40.

     10. M. K. Guzda, "Billy Graham to Newspapers: Cover Religion News Better," ibid., 11 May 1985, pp. 30, 48.

     11. "Rarity in the News: A TV Station Takes Religion Seriously," *Christianity Today,* 20 November 1981, pp. 52–53.

     12. "The Religion Beat: The Reporting of Religion in the Media," Rockefeller Foundation, conference report, 1981; Terry Mattingly, "Religion News: No Room at the Inn?" *Quill,* January 1983, pp. 12–19; William C. Simbro, "Unheralded Religion News," *Quill,* December 1979, pp. 11–14, 23; Gary Wills, "The Greatest Story Ever Told," *Columbia Journalism Review,* January/February 1980, pp. 25–33.

     13. Michael Novak, "Television Shapes the Soul," in Adler, *Understanding Television,* p. 31.

     14. Joseph P. Duggan, "Is the Media's Language a 'Marxist Vulgate'?" *Vital Speeches of the Day,* 1 August 1981, pp. 635–37.

     15. David B. Liroff, "A Comparative Content Analysis of Network Television Evening News Programs and Other National News Media in the United States" (Ph.D. diss., Northwestern Univ., 1970), p. 170.

     16. James F. Larson, *Television's Window on the World: International Affairs Coverage on the U.S. Networks* (Norwood, N.J.: Ablex, 1984), pp. 55–56.

     17. Echo Ellen Fields, "Preachers, Press, and Politics: The Media Career of a Conservative Social Movement" (Ph.D. diss., Univ. of Oregon, 1984), pp. iv–v, 341–57.

     18. Joanmarie Kalter, "The Greatest Stories Never Told . . . Right," reprint from *TV Guide,* 16 November 1985.

     19. Dan Nimmo and James E. Combs, *Nightly Horrors: Crisis Coverage by Television Network News* (Knoxville: Univ. of Tennessee Press, 1985), pp. 32–59, 140–78.

20. Ole R. Holsti, *Content Analysis for the Social Sciences and Humanities* (Reading, Mass.: Addison-Wesley, 1969), p. 134.

21. The Equal Opportunities Council of Colorado State University provided funds for this research.


## 5: Religious Television Spots

1. J. Harold Ellens, *Models of Religious Broadcasting* (Grand Rapids, Mich.: William B. Eerdmans, 1974), p. 132.

2. "How Humor 'Sells' Religion on TV," *Broadcasting,* 2 August 1965, p. 36.

3. Peter G. Horsfield, *Religious Television: The American Experience* (New York: Longman, 1984), pp. 3–7.

4. Ibid., p. 9.

5. "Church Messages Rate High in Remembrance," *Editor & Publisher,* 8 January 1966, p. 17.

6. Horsfield, *Religious Television,* p. 9.

7. Edward J. Carnell, *Television: Servant or Master?* (Grand Rapids, Mich.: William B. Eerdmans, 1950), p. 93.

8. Ellens, *Models of Religious Broadcasting,* p. 127.

9. Clayton T. Griswold and Charles H. Schmitz, comps., *How You Can Broadcast Religion* (New York: Broadcasting and Film Commission, National Council of the Churches of Christ in the United States of America, 1957), pp. 52–53.

10. Ellens, *Models of Religious Broadcasting,* pp. 123–24.

11. Ibid., p. 124.

12. "Heavenly Commercials," *Newsweek,* 30 October 1967, pp. 57–58.

13. Charles Brackbill, Jr., "The Church Must Use Television," *Religion in Life* 22 (Winter 1952–53): 117.

14. "And When the Churches Themselves Advertise," *Madison Avenue,* September 1985, p. 106.

15. Ibid.

16. Ibid.

17. Terry Ann Knopf, "Advertising for Priests," *Boston Globe,* 24 March 1980, pp. 21–22.

18. Martin E. Marty, "Cultivating Bad Taste," *Christian Century,* 12 November 1986, p. 1015.

19. Razelle Frankl, *Televangelism: The Marketing of Popular Religion* (Carbondale: Southern Illinois Univ. Press, 1987), p. 99.

20. Larry Hollon, "Selling Human Misery," *Christian Century,* 26 October 1983, pp. 968–71.

21. "Celebrities Featured in Baptists' Texas Drive," *Advertising Age,* 28 February 1977, p. 35.

22. William Martin, "The Baptists Want You!" *Texas Monthly,* February 1977, p. 84.

23. James M. Palmer and Janet S. Palmer, "Good News Texas: A Study of Intensive Evangelism through Media and the Churches" (East Texas Baptist College, 1978, unpublished report), p. 4.

24. Ibid., pp. 25, 47, and 140.

25. Randy Frame, "Millions Respond to National Evangelistic Media Blitz," *Christianity Today,* 3 February 1984, pp. 40, 43.

26. Stephen W. McDaniel, "Church Advertising: Views of the Clergy and General Public," *Journal of Advertising* 15 (1986): 24–29.

27. "Lutherans Pleased with Ad Test; Plan More Inclusive Body," *Advertising Age,* 17 January 1966, p. 40.

28. Cherie L. Nagy, "Use the Airwaves to Publicize Your Church," *Christianity Today,* 17 November 1978, p. 30.

29. Independent Broadcasting Authority, *The IBA Code of Advertising Standards and Practice* (London: IBA, 1987), p. 3.

30. Reinhold Niebuhr, "What Are the Churches Advertising?" *Christian Century,* 27 November 1926, p. 1533.

31. Virginia Stem Owens, *The Total Image, or Selling Jesus in the Modern Age* (Grand Rapids, Mich.: William B. Eerdmans, 1980), pp. 24–25, 34.

32. Malcolm Muggeridge, *Christ and the Media* (Grand Rapids, Mich.: William B. Eerdmans, 1977), p. 12.

33. Neil Postman, *Amusing Ourselves to Death: Public Discourse in the Age of Show Business* (New York: Viking, 1985), pp. 117, 120.

34. John Whale, *The Half-Shut Eye: Television and Politics in Britain and America* (London: Macmillan, 1969), p. 154.

35. Ellens, *Models of Religious Broadcasting,* p. 132.

36. L. W. Michaelson, "Religion and Madison Avenue," *Catholic World,* August 1955, p. 376.

37. A. William Bluem, *Religious Television Programs: A Study of Relevance* (New York: Hastings House, 1969), p. 185.

38. H. Richard Niebuhr, *Christ and Culture* (New York: Harper & Row, 1951).

39. Ellens, *Models of Religious Broadcasting,* p. 125.

40. Ibid.

41. "Spots for God," *Time,* 12 January 1970, pp. 33, 35.

42. Jack Wintz, "Telespots: Marketing the Message," *St. Anthony Messenger,* September 1973, p. 23.

43. Alfred Loisy, *The Gospel and the Church,* trans. Christopher Home (London: Isbister, 1903).

44. Dennis C. Benson, *Electric Evangelism* (Nashville: Abingdon, 1973), p. 113.

45. Erik Barnouw, *The Sponsor: Notes on a Modern Potentate* (New York: Oxford Univ. Press, 1978), pp. 140–46.

46. Ellens, *Models of Religious Broadcasting,* p. 134.

47. "National Church Group Tests Spot TV Ads in Ohio," *Advertising Age,* 7 March 1966, p. 20.

48. "No Spot for God," *Newsweek,* 25 July 1966, p. 84.
49. The College of Arts and Sciences at the University of Louisville supported this study with a research grant.


## 6: Religious Watchdog Groups and Prime-Time Programming

1. Reinhold Niebuhr, Introduction to Wilbur Schramm, *Responsibility in Mass Communication* (New York: Harper & Brothers, 1957), p. xv.
2. Samuel 1:20 is only one ancient example.
3. Ann Ilan Alter, "An Introduction to the Exhibition," in *Censorship: 500 Years of Conflict* (New York: Oxford Univ. Press, 1984), pp. 16–17.
4. The International Reform Federation, Inc., is now led by Samuel A. Jeanes, pastor of the First Baptist Church of Merchantville, New Jersey. A recent issue of its publication, *Progress,* carries articles about drunkenness, tobacco, AIDS, drug addiction, lotteries, and children's television. The group's historic motto has not changed: "To promote those moral and social reforms on which the churches generally agree."
5. Catheryne Cooke Gilman, "Government Regulation for the Movies," *Christian Century,* 26 August 1931, p. 1066.
6. Morris Ernst and Pare Lorentz, *Censored: The Private Life of the Movies* (New York: Jonathan Cape and Harrison Smith, 1930), p. 199.
7. T. O. Boyle, "We Are All Censors," *Commonweal,* 21 December 1934, p. 227.
8. Religious concern about radio was directed mostly toward the production of religious programs. Only one watchdog, the Joint Religious Radio Committee (JRRC), founded by Everett Parker in 1944, took initiative in the public arena and argued, among other things, for the public interest standard before the Federal Communications Commission. In 1948 the Protestant Radio Commission of the Federal Council of Churches of Christ (FCCC) merged with the JRRC. Then in 1950 the FCCC became the National Council of the Churches of Christ in the United States of America (NCC). Its Broadcasting and Film Commission began to handle all cooperative Protestant programming. At about the same time, the American Council of Churches (1941) and the National Association of Evangelicals (1942) began efforts to cut into network public service time dominated by the FCCC. Also, the Southern Religious Radio Conference (SRRC, organized in 1945) represented interests of Southern Baptist, Lutheran, Methodist, Presbyterian USA, and Protestant Episcopal churches.
9. The NCCPV report included in its fifteen volumes the

report by Robert K. Baker and Sandra J. Ball, *Violence and the Media.*

10. *Television and Growing Up: The Impact of Televised Violence* (Washington, D.C.: U.S. Government Printing Office, 1971.)

11. Todd Gitlin suggests that the 1960s changed America from a consensus to a special-interest culture. "Scarcely a social group was willing to rest content with its position" (p. 249). See Gitlin, *Inside Prime Time* (New York: Pantheon, 1983), chap. 12.

12. Joseph Turow draws an important distinction between public and audience in "Pressure Groups and Television Entertainment" in Willard D. Rowland, Jr., and Bruce Watkins, eds., *Interpreting Television: Current Research Perspectives* (Beverly Hills, Calif.: Sage, 1984), pp. 142–62. That networks worry over audiences while monitors worry over publics accounts for much of the cross talk between the two groups, Turow argues.

13. Stewart Hoover argues that the UCC campaign generated the media reform movement, in *The Electronic Giant* (Elgin, Ill.: Brethren Press, 1982).

14. Fred W. Friendly, *The Good Guys, the Bad Guys, and the First Amendment* (New York: Vintage, 1977), chap. 7.

15. *Office of Communication of the United Church of Christ v. FCC,* 359 F.2d 994 (1966); *United Church of Christ v. FCC,* 425 F.2d 543 (1969).

16. *Weekly Television Digest,* 29 November 1976, p. 5.

17. These resolutions and a summary of the movement in the mid-1970s are included in Freedom of Information Center Report no. 416, School of Journalism, University of Missouri–Columbia, 1980.

18. *New York Times,* 27 June 1977, p. 53; ibid., 12 July 1977, p. 59.

19. *Christian Science Monitor,* 15 August 1977.

20. Clifford G. Christians, Kim B. Rotzoll, and Mark Fackler, *Media Ethics: Cases and Moral Reasoning* (New York: Longman, 1983), p. 277.

21. To the credit of the United Church of Christ and the United Methodist Church, but fully in keeping with the gentle efforts of the mainstream monitors, the series "Six American Families" was shown in the spring of 1977 on PBS and Group W. The series featured families from different socioeconomic and ethnic backgrounds, to "illustrate through persons living today the moral fortitude that has been America's greatest strength and most precious asset" (Everett Parker, quoted in Freedom of Information Center Report no. 416). The obvious contrast between the noble goals of the UCC-UMC family series and the comedic-satirical goals of the ABC "family" sitcom may partially explain the coalition's firm but gentle protest: those who produce television are most sensitive to the difficulties of producing good television.

22. *New York Times,* 27 June 1977, p. 53.

23. *Morality in Media Newsletter,* November 1977, p. 4.

24. Gitlin, *Inside Prime Time,* p. 250.

25. *Christianity Today,* 30 December 1977, p. 42.

26. *Commonweal,* 11 November 1977, p. 723; *Newsweek,* 13 June 1977, p. 92.

27. "Forces Combating TV Smut Flex Their New Muscle," *Christianity Today,* 13 March 1981, p. 74.

28. "Threat of TV Boycott Wrings Concessions from the Networks," ibid., 7 August 1981, p. 46.

29. Of particular concern in the NBC schedule was the series "Love Sidney" about a middle-aged, inactive homosexual who keeps company with an unwed mother and her child.

30. Gregory D. Warner, "Morals in the Marketplace: The TV Coalition in Context," *Christian Century,* 13 April 1983, p. 344.

31. Quoted in "Threat of TV Boycott," p. 46.

32. Conversation with Donald Wildmon, 14 July 1987. The precise nature of the data and a host of related questions about the training of monitors, the reliability and validity of the results, and the system by which sponsors are ranked in each category remain guarded information.

33. Conversation with Mark Taylor, 20 July 1987.

34. Memo entitled "Why the National Board of CLeaR-TV Decided to Take This Action," n.d.

35. Conversation with Ralph Daniel of NBC, 3 August 1987.

36. *NAE Insight,* July 1987, p. 3.

37. Conversation with Donald Wildmon, 14 July 1987.

38. *NAE Insight,* October 1987, p. 3.

39. Donald Wildmon, "A Time for Decision," *Religious Broadcasting,* April 1982, p. 27.

40. Ibid., p. 24.

41. Fundamentalists read the book of Daniel as predictive and thus believe that a second great invasion of the restored Israelite Temple will signal the final stages of history's end.

42. Correspondence with John P. Blessington, Alfred R. Schneider, and Ralph Daniels.

43. The article is by Gary Selnow, "Solving Problems on Prime-Time Television," *Journal of Communication* 36 (Spring 1986): 63–72, quotation, p. 71.

44. Arthur Schlesinger, Jr., *Censorship: 500 Years of Conflict* (New York: Oxford Univ. Press, 1984), p. 7.

45. Ibid.

46. C. Wright Mills, *The Power Elite* (New York: Oxford Univ. Press, 1956), pp. 306–11.

47. Jacques Ellul, *The Political Illusion,* trans. Konrad Kellar (New York: Vintage, 1967), p. 217.

48. Robert Bellah et al., *Habits of the Heart: Individualism and Commitment in American Life* (Berkeley: Univ. of California Press, 1985).

49. Stanley Hauerwas, *A Community of Character* (Notre Dame: Univ. of Notre Dame Press, 1981).

50. For a more detailed recital of the meaning of this phrase, see Clifford G. Christians and Mark Fackler, "Liberty within the Bounds of Virtue," in Anne van der Meiden, ed., *Ethics and Mass Communication* (Utrecht, Netherlands: Department of Mass Communications, University of Utrecht, 1980), pp. 16–41.

51. H. Richard Niebuhr, *Christ and Culture* (New York: Harper & Row, 1951). William Fore makes the same point in his *Television and Religion: The Shaping of Faith, Values, and Culture* (Minneapolis: Augsburg, 1987), p. 34

# INDEX